CW00684732

LOST RACE TRACKS

TREASURES OF AUTOMOTIVE RACING

Gordon Eliot White

Iconografix

Iconografix
PO Box 446
Hudson, Wisconsin 54016 USA

© 2002 Gordon E. White

All rights reserved. No part of this work may be reproduced or used in any form by any means... graphic, electronic, or mechanical, including photocopying, recording, taping, or any other information storage and retrieval system... without written permission of the publisher.

The information in this book is true and complete to the best of our knowledge. All recommendations are made without any guarantee on the part of the author or Publisher, who also disclaim any liability incurred in connection with the use of this data or specific details.

We acknowledge that certain words, such as model names and designations, mentioned herein are the property of the trademark holder. We use them for purposes of identification only. This is not an official publication.

Iconografix books are offered at a discount when sold in quantity for promotional use. Businesses or organizations seeking details should write to the Marketing Department, Iconografix, at the above address.

Library of Congress Card Number: 2002112569

ISBN 1-58388-084-4

03 04 05 06 07 08 09 5 4 3 2 1

Printed in China

Cover and book design by Shawn Glidden

Copyediting by Suzie Helberg

Cover photo: see page 27

BOOK PROPOSALS

Iconografix is a publishing company specializing in books for transportation enthusiasts. We publish in a number of different areas, including Automobiles, Auto Racing, Buses, Construction Equipment, Emergency Equipment, Farming Equipment, Railroads & Trucks. The Iconografix imprint is constantly growing and expanding into new subject areas.

Authors, editors, and knowledgeable enthusiasts in the field of transportation history are invited to contact the Editorial Department at Iconografix, Inc., PO Box 446, Hudson, WI 54016.

TABLE OF CONTENTS

DEDICATION

Bruce Craig was a gifted photographer of auto racing for nearly fifty years. He and Vincente Alvarez purchased and preserved a score of the best racing collections from around the world. A generation of racing writers and historians will forever be in his debt. This book and dozens of others could not have been created without him. *Photo: Bruce Craig, 1938-2001*

ACKNOWLEDGMENTS

This book could not have been written, nor the photographs and maps found, without help from a great many people. Of immense help were my colleagues, Allan Brown, author of *America's Speedways*, the definitive list of virtually all of the racetracks that have ever existed in the U.S. and Canada, and Harold Osmer, author of *Where They Raced*, a detailed compendium of Southern California racetracks, as well as books on road racing and the Saugus Speedway. The staff of the Geography and Map Division of the Library of Congress were unfailingly helpful and cheerful as I asked them to bring scores of maps from their stacks. Likewise, Robert Beir and Nora Tamberg at the United States Geological Survey Library went above and beyond to find maps that were not in the standard indexes.

The death of my other colleague, Bruce Craig, at a critical juncture in late November 2001, was a great loss to history and placed a great burden on other friends who stepped into the breach when Bruce's collection was no longer accessible. His wife, Jeanne, and successor, Dale Snyder, did their best to help me get what was available from existing prints that Bruce left behind.

Joe Freeman, Phil Harms, Tom Saal, Joe Heisler, Tommy Caruso, Dick Wallen, Mike Bell and Len Ashburn were among several friends who gave me photographs from their collections that were not available elsewhere.

In general, America's librarians and historical society archivists were of inestimable value to this project, showing unusual interest in a subject many of them had never thought much about before. I believe many non-racing folk were amazed to find that Will Pickens, Barney Oldfield and Lincoln Beachy had raced at their local fairgrounds nearly a century ago.

Among those who helped were: Jeff Adams, Bill Akin, Ruth Anderson, Andy Anderson, Don Anderson, Richard Andre, Bob Armstrong, Ed Asbury, Linda Bailey, Larry Ball, Bob Barkheimer, Joe Bauman, Hugo Becker, Mike Bell, Charles Betts, Arlyn Booth, Alden Bopp, Fred Brucker, Dave Burt, LeRoy Byers, Betty Carlan, Roy Carlson, Jim Carmichael, Cheshire Fair, Maj. Michael Clark, Ken Coles, Jim Collins, Thomas Conaway, Cynthia Cook, Jim Stanley, Jim Corbin, Harrison Cornet, Frank Crosby, Wilson Davis, Ed de Brecht, Robert Deull, Phyllis Devine, Marian Dinwiddie, Jim Dobbs, Beryl Doyle, J. W. Dunlop, Jack Dyer, Maria Eckhoff, Chris Economaki, Kathryn Engstrom, Gene Erickson, Jim Etter, Dale Fairfax, Bob Falcon, Jim Fisher, Jim Flatness, Jeff Gamble, Jim Gerber, Larry Giles, Keith Gill, Scott Gosse, Brad Gray, Bill Green, Dr. Ronald Grim, Roger Grupp, Ole Gudmundson, Carl Halberg, Kandace Hankinson, Larry Harrison, John Hebert, Mary Ann Heydenreich, Bill Hill, Marty Himes, Mike Holland, Carol Holzer, Hooker Hood, Paul Hoof, Billy Horner, Deke Houlgate, Charlotte Houtz, Mike Hunter, Roger Hurst, Walt Imlay, Alan Isselhard, Jeff Iula, Larry Janisek, Larry Jendras, Ken Johnson, Walt Jorgensen, Brian Katen, David Kennedy, Les King, Mary Klatt, Michael Klein, Charles Klem, Tom Konop, Earl Krause, George Laughead, Bill Lawler, Bob Lawrence, Herb Lederer, Marty Little, Don Litzer, Stanley Lobitz, Al Longe, Susan Lowell, Ray Lustig, Michael Lynch, John Mahoney, Bob Manley, Tony Martin, Jack Martin, Jerry Massey, Bob Mays, Bob McConnell, Buz McKim, Ken McMaken, Charles McQuien, Dave Michaels, Joe Michalek, Bill Miller, Kim Miller, Dick Morris, Tom Motter, Jerry Murawski, Joel Naprstek, Milton Ogden, John Oyler, Jim O'Keefe, Stephen Paczolt, Stephen Paschen, Tom Paul, Wayne Petersen, Lee Pierce, Brian Pratt, Fred Probst, Leslie Przybylek, Don Radbruch, Robert Rampton, Mitch Rasansky, Mary Rayson, Edward Redmond, Terry Reed, Troy Reeves, John Reilly, Dave Reininger, Ruth Renz, Judy Riggs, Mike Ringo, Bill Rinke, Ernie Roberson, Kem Robertson, Eddie Roche, Dave Roethel, Steve Rogers, Thomas Rooney, Robert Rowe, Butch Salter, Gerald Santibanes, Tom Savage, Richard Sayen, Mary Jane Schmalz, Tom Schmeh, Janice Scott, David Scully, Bob Sheldon, Bob Shelton, R. A. Silvia, Dan Simeone, Glenn Starbeck, Don Stauffer, Mark Steigerwald, Karen Stevens, Bob Storck, Les Swanson, Jim Taggart, Habte Teclemariam, Jim Thurman, Celeste Tibbetts, Jane Townsend, Bob Tronolone, Steve Truchan, Bobby Unser, Fred Usher, Roy Valasek, Amy Von Walter, Ron Watson, Joe Westervelt, Matt Weston, Jesse White, Angela White, Kathy Wilhelm, D. Willett, Steve Williams, Pam Williams, Crocky Wright, Steve Zautke, Cpt. Channing Zucker.

INTRODUCTION

Racetracks can be as evanescent as the mile-and-a-quarter board speedway at Fulford-by-the-Sea, Florida, which was destroyed by a hurricane in 1926 after a single race, or as permanent as the New York State Fairgrounds in Syracuse, built as a horse track in 1880, first used by cars in 1903 and still going strong. Between those extremes nearly 7,000 racecourses are known to have existed in the United States during the 107 years of organized motorsports. Of those, about 1,200—fewer than 20 percent—still run.

The tracks that have come and gone represent a sport which is pure Americana; oval tracks and drag strips, with a sprinkling of road courses of the sort so popular in Europe. Some, like Riverside and Atlantic City, were built with great fanfare for millions of dollars. Others were dirt strips, scraped out of a Midwest cornfield or a New Jersey pasture that ran for only a year or two. Most were built by enthusiasts who loved racing and took less than a close look at the financial bottom line. Some were, in effect, real estate holding operations, just waiting for a more lucrative use such as a housing development or shopping mall.

Most of us can recall, with nostalgia, the tracks where we first watched auto racing, racing the way we feel it should still be today, on "real dirt." Or on the boards, with engines in front of the driver, without "wings" —even the winged, rear-engine cars of the past 25 years. Like many of man's creations, these tracks have come and passed away, dust into dust become.

I have used maps to indicate where the tracks were located. Some of these maps are faded and indistinct, but are the best that survive today. Outside of major cities the U.S. was not well mapped until World War II. Most of the maps in this book are from the U.S. Geological Survey. Some are from the Sanborn insurance maps in the Library of Congress. A few are promotional drawings by the track operators.

I have tried to present in this book a cross-section of those 5,800 lost tracks across America. Chronologically these tracks range from the Times-Herald racecourse in Chicago that had a single event in 1895, to Shangri La, in New York State, that closed in 2001.

Looking at the tracks that have disappeared, or ceased running auto races, a few patterns are obvious. The public's taste in entertainment has changed. Just as eight-day bicycle racing and harness racing faded in the face of the more-exciting thrills of auto racing, so some audiences, particularly at the fairgrounds, have become more interested in country music and rock band performers. Sound stages have gone up on racetracks. Other tracks have given up in the face of costs for safety improvements such as guardrails and catch fences, and ever-increasing insurance premiums. But the two largest causes of racetracks disappearing are poor finances and the escalating value of the real estate. As one promoter said recently, "They hardly ever tear down a shopping center to build a racetrack."

I have tried to find photographs that show what each track and its grandstands looked like when they were in use for motor racing. Many of the photographs are snapshots from old scrapbooks and a few are from faded newspaper clippings. Little caption information was available for some of them, particularly those that were discovered in the collections of local libraries and historical societies. They are a nostalgic glance into the past. I hope they give a flavor of the age when brave men and a few women raced, wheel to wheel, on dirt, cinders, and asphalt, concrete or wood, to glory or sometimes to death.

ABBREVIATIONS

In this book I have described racing cars of less than championship level, and not midgets, as "big cars," because that is the way they were usually described in the years when many of these tracks were in operation. The term "sprint cars" became common after 1950.

I have often used initials for the organizations that sanction auto racing:

AAA	the Contest Board of the American Automobile Association, 1908-1955
AARC	Atlantic Auto Racing Association
ACRA	Atlantic Coast Racing Association
AMRA	American Motor Racing Association
ARA	American Racing Association (northeastern area midgets)
ARCA	Auto Racing Association of America, 1934-1941
ARDC	The American Racing Drivers Club, 1939-
BSRA	Bay State Auto Racing Association
CART	Championship Auto Racing Teams
CORA	Car Owners Racing Association
CSRA	Central State Racing Association
GSRA	Garden State Racing Association
HHRA	Hurricane Hot Rod Association
IMCA	International Motor Contest Association
IMSA	International Motor Sports Association
IRA	Interstate Racing Association
MDTRA	Midwest Dirt Track Racing Association
MRA	Metropolitan Racing Association
NASCAR	National Association for Stock Car Auto Racing
NEARA	New England Auto Racing Association
NEMA	Northeastern Midget Racing Association
NMRA	National Motor Racing Association
NMRA	New Mexico Racing Association
SCCA	Sports Car Club of America
SCODA	Sports car Owners & Drivers Association
SCTA	Southern California Timing Association
SMRC	Super Midget Racing Association
TRA	Triangle Auto Racing Association
UMRC	United Midget Racing Club
URA	United Racing Association
URC	United Racing Club
USAC	United States Auto Club, 1956-

Iron Bowl, Birmingham, Alabama

The Iron Bowl, which took its name from the steel industry in nearby Birmingham, was a 3/8-mile dirt track carved out of Boggs Hollow, a natural valley in the hills between Roebuck and Robinwood, in 1939. IMCA "big cars" ran there occasionally but the racing after World War II was first "independent" and then the NASCAR short-track division. Jerry Massey, of Southside, Alabama was one of the stars, winning 37 races over the years. The track closed in 1961 when local racing moved to the fairgrounds in Bessemer, Alabama.

Photo: International Motorsports Hall of Fame
Map: 1959

Iron Bowl 1949

Arizona State Fairgrounds, Phoenix, Arizona

The Arizona State Fairgrounds, at McDowell Road and 19th Avenue, in Phoenix, was the terminus for the Cactus Derby, which began in 1908, but the first race on the 1-mile dirt track itself came in 1910. A 5/8-mile paved track was built inside the mile in 1939 and hosted racing until a spectator fatality in 1972. Phoenix was, for more than half a century, a stop on the Championship Trail of the old American Automobile Association. Jimmy Bryan won the final AAA 100-mile race here on November 6, 1955. USAC and other racing continued at Phoenix until 1964, when the championship races were shifted to the paved Phoenix International Raceway. There was, for a time, a 1/8-mile track at the Fairgrounds, which, themselves, survive.

Photo: Phil Harms

Map: 1952

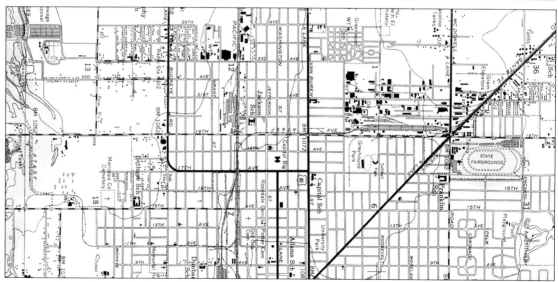

Jenny Lind Track, Fort Smith, Arkansas

Fort Smith built a typical 1/2-mile fairground race-track at Jenny Lind Road and South 20th Street in 1911. Local citizens ran timed laps at the first Arkansas-Oklahoma Fair on October 17. Barney Oldfield and Will Pickens had run on an earlier Ft. Smith track in 1910 and Oldfield returned in 1914 and set "a new world's record" on the Jenny Lind track. The photograph shows Oldfield in the Winton Bullet II circling the track on his record run. IMCA and independent groups raced at the Jenny Lind track during the Depression and for several years after World War II. Midgets ran there at least a half-dozen times in 1947. Around 1952 the site was cleared for construction of the Fairview and Ramsey schools.

Photo: Fort Smith Museum of History

Map: 1951

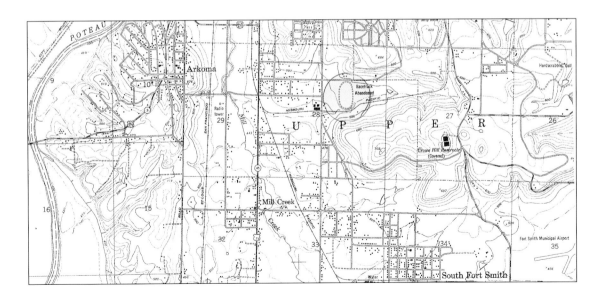

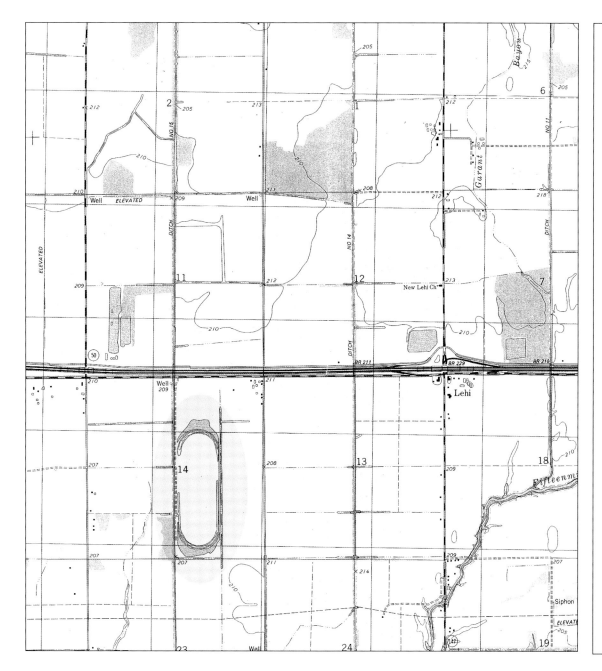

Memphis-Arkansas Speedway, Lehi, Arkansas

In 1953 two contractors and a pawnshop operator built a high-banked 1 1/2-mile dirt track just west of the hamlet of Lehi, Arkansas, on U.S. Route 70, 18 miles from Memphis. At the time NASCAR was expanding and Lehi became one of the stops on the Grand National stock car circuit. The track was originally to have been paved, but the owners could not afford the $100,000 price for asphalt. Later a 1/4-mile dirt track was added in the infield for local short-track races. Hooker Hood, a Memphis racing legend, started on the outside of the first row in the first Modified race on October 9, 1954, and led until a tie rod broke. Buck Baker, in an Oldsmobile, won the next day's main event, the Mid-South 250, before a crowd of 10,000.

In 1955 Lehi saw two NASCAR races. Dust was an immediate problem.

In 1956 two drivers died at Lehi, Clint McHugh and Cotton Priddy, both on the same race weekend in June. The track held its last NASCAR race on July 14, 1957. The owners sold the 160-acre tract to Layton Eubanks, a local farmer. Ponds in the infield were used to raise catfish and one "mud race" was later held for charity.

The big oval outline of the track remains to this day while the Eubanks grow rice in the infield of what might have become a NASCAR superspeedway if dust and the weather had not spoiled so many of its races.

Map: 1981

Ascot Motor Speedway, Los Angeles, California

Legion Ascot Speedway, built in 1924 on Valley Boulevard at Soto Street on the Los Angeles-Alhambra boundary, was a 5/8-mile banked track of oiled dirt. After it failed to make money for several promoters, the Glendale American Legion post took it over and made it a success, both on the track and at the box office. For one 1934 event a 1.385-mile road course was laid out in the hills beyond the backstretch.

Ascot was by far the most successful American track in the Depression years of the 1930s, but a succession of fatal accidents brought opposition from the Los Angeles newspapers. A final crash in February 1936 that killed Al Gordon and Spider Matlock forced its closing.

Photo: Bruce Craig

Map: 1935

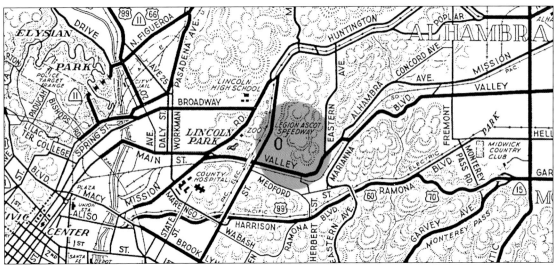

Cactus Derby, California-Arizona

In November 1908, the Mariocopa County, Arizona, Auto Club held the first of what they called the "Cactus Derby," a road race from Los Angeles to Phoenix over abandoned stagecoach trails. The route involved crossing the Colorado River on a log raft. The 1908 winner, Col. F. C. Fenners and his mechanic, H. D. Ryus, in a White Steamer took 29 hours and 26 minutes to negotiate the 455-mile course.

In 1909, under AAA sanction, ten cars competed over a 480-mile route, slightly longer but quite a bit faster as Joe and Louis Nikrent won in a Buick in 19 hours 13 minutes.

The race continued until 1914 as seen in the photographs. The event finished at the Phoenix Fairgrounds. Barney Oldfield won the final Cactus Derby in a Stutz at an average speed of 29 mph, for which he was awarded a medal proclaiming him "The Master Driver of the World."

Photos: AACA Library

Map: 1908

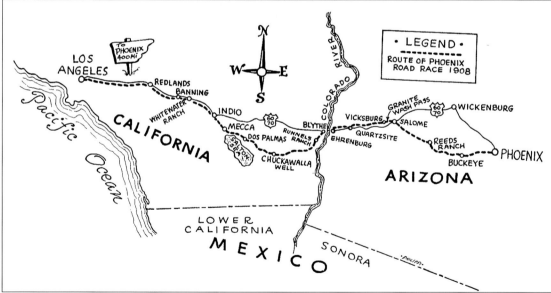

Corona, California

When the City of Corona was planned in 1896, the founders laid out its main street as a perfect circle one mile in diameter. In 1913, with road racing highly successful at Santa Monica, Grand Boulevard made a perfect street-racing venue, 2.77 miles in circumference. A $10,000 purse attracted top cars and drivers for the first race on September 9, which Earl Cooper won in a Stutz.

A year later, on Thanksgiving Day, Eddie Pullen won in a Mercer before a throng of 150,000. Corona's third and final race came on April 8, 1916. Bob Burman, seen here in the upper photo with his Peugeot (just extensively re-worked by Harry A. Miller), crashed to his death along with Eric Schroeder, his riding mechanic, and a track policeman.

Today Grand Boulevard still circles Corona, though Route 91 has sliced off its northern arc.

Photos: W. A. Hughes
Map: 1930

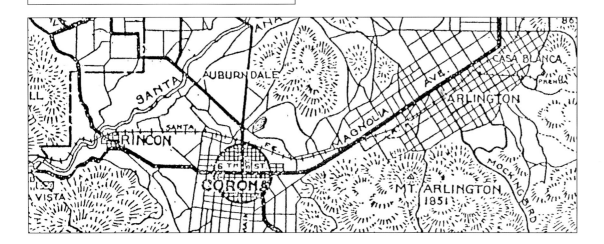

Gilmore Stadium, Los Angeles, California

Gilmore Stadium, built in 1934 on Beverly Boulevard by oil magnate Earl Gilmore, was the first track specifically designed for the newly popular midgets. Its 1/5-mile (expanded to a quarter-mile in 1936) surface of crushed granite was nearly perfect, creating little dust and not packing into a slick hardpan during an evening's races.

The first Offenhauser engine was tested at Gilmore and the first midget fatality, to Chet Mortemore, came here on October 25, 1934. It was the top midget track in race-crazy Southern California and its graduates went on to win at Indianapolis seven times.

In 1950 CBS bought the land for its Los Angeles Television City studio. Bill Zaring won the final Gilmore Grand Prix on November 23, 1950. On this map the Gilmore soccer field, the Pan-Pacific Auditorium and the Los Angeles County Farmers' Market are still standing. Today the Farmers' Market is the only vestige of the days of Gilmore and the mighty midgets.

Upper photo: Bruce Craig
Lower photo: Harold Osmer
Map: 1953

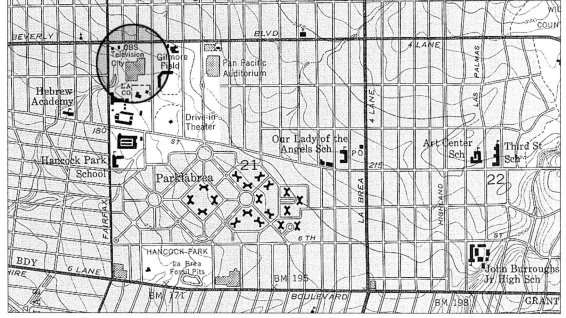

Los Angeles Coliseum, California

The Los Angeles Memorial Coliseum was built in 1923 at 3939 South Figueroa Street on the site of the old Agricultural Park (1908-1921), which had been a dirt oval converted to a board track for motorcycles. The area was re-named Exposition Park and the Coliseum was the University of Southern California's football stadium. Seating 90,000 fans, it hosted the 1932 Summer Olympics. It would later see the 1984 Olympics, two Super Bowls, a World Series and a visit from the Pope. It is one of two auto racetracks to be designated a National Historic Landmark.

At the end of World War II promoter Bill White installed a quarter-mile paved track where the URA held wildly popular midget races before crowds that reached more than 55,000. Midget driver Sport Briggs was killed in the opening race.

When attendance began to drop in July 1948, White built a $125,000 board track. The highly banked boards were about 12 miles an hour faster than the nearly flat asphalt, but slicker and harder to drive.

With attendance slipping, White held the Coliseum's last race on Friday, August 13, 1948. Tragedy struck on that unlucky night as Jack Habermehl hit Bob Kelsey's car, which had lost a wheel and went end over end. Habermehl was dead upon arrival at Parkview Hospital and so was auto racing at the Coliseum. White had held 32 races there over a four-year period.

Photo: Bruce Craig

Map: 1953

Muroc Dry Lake, California

Californians were driving fast cars on the hard alkali flats of Rodgers Dry Lake at Muroc, 60 miles north of Los Angeles, as early as 1910. AAA-sanctioned speed attempts began there in 1923. Los Angeles hot rodders soon followed, with the first organized meet held in 1931.

In 1933 Lt. Col. "Hap" Arnold chose Muroc as a training site for his Army Air Corps squadron at March Field and in 1935 the legendary Pancho Barnes built the Happy Bottom Riding Club bar on the other side of the lakebed. There was enough room for the fliers, Barnes, and the racecars until World War II, when the Air Corps vastly expanded its facilities.

In this photo AAA Starter Fred Wagner gives Tommy Milton the green flag for a run at Muroc on April 4, 1924 with a Miller 183. Milton went 151.260 mph, a record for a 3-litre car. Frank Lockhart turned a 171.020 mph run with a blown Miller 91 speedway car in 1927.

In 1949 Muroc was re-named Edwards Air Force Base and the lakebed re-christened Rogers Lake. Barnes and the hot rodders were evicted. Even the Santa Fe Railroad tracks were shifted to the north, as America needed a place to test exotic, high-speed aircraft. In the 1990s the Air Force permitted the hot rodders to return to Muroc to hold a nostalgia meet.

Photo: Mark Dees Collection
Map: 1942

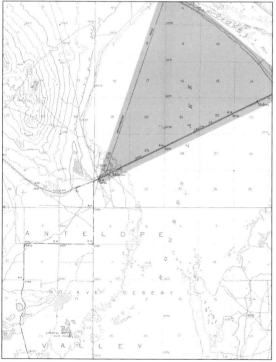

17

Oakland Speedway/Stadium, San Leandro, California

The old Oakland Speedway, on Hesperian Boulevard and 14th Street in San Leandro, was built in 1931. It was, as shown in the photograph, a 1-mile dirt track. The stands burned down in the winter of 1941-'42 and the track was abandoned. After the war, a new track, known as Oakland Stadium, was built on the same site. (The map-markers did not notice the name change, which by 1948 was no longer "Speedway.")

That high-banked paved, 5/8-mile track was a fast, exciting place. Troy Ruttman set a record of 116 mph there in 1950. So steep were the banks that the centrifugal force would collapse wheels. There was also a quarter-mile track built inside the larger oval where the BCRA midgets raced. Oakland's last race was held in 1955, after which the stadium was demolished to make way for the $25 million Bay-Fair shopping center.

Photo: Bruce Craig

Map: 1948

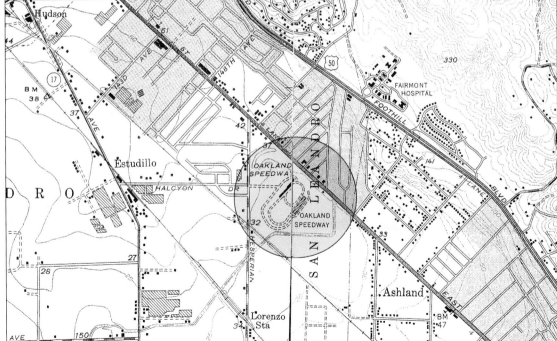

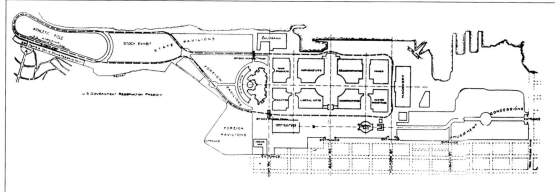

Panama-Pacific International Exposition Course, San Francisco, California

The site of San Francisco's Panama-Pacific International Exposition of 1915 was the shoreline of San Francisco Bay, from Hamilton Street at the Presidio to Laguna Street, in what became the Marina District. Much of the land was built on pilings and fill. A track at the Presidio had been used for races since 1909, but in 1915 it was expanded to a 3.95-mile road course, around the stadium track and among lavish palm-lined avenues between the Moorish-style pavilions. Turns were paved with wood to prevent the cars from running into the stone curbs.

The San Francisco weather, despite optimistic predictions, was awful and it rained during the "Sixth American Grand Prix," contested by drivers such as Barney Oldfield in a Maxwell, Earl Cooper in a Stutz and Eddie Rickenbacker in another Maxwell.

The photograph shows the cars thundering down the rain-drenched course past the foreign exposition pavilions on the first lap of the Grand Prix. Englishman Dario Resta won both the 400-mile road race on February 27th and the 300-mile 1915 Vanderbilt Cup contest on March 6th in a Peugeot, then edging out American Howdy Wilcox in a Stutz Bearcat. There are reports that a race of some sort was run at the site as late as 1940, but of the buildings only the Palace of Fine Arts, reconstructed in the 1960s, remains. The stadium site was later occupied by Crissy Army Airfield.

Photo: Smithsonian
Map: 1915

Pebble Beach, California

Pebble Beach was a high-toned resort long before sports car road racing began at Watkins Glen. Not to be outdone, in 1951 California aficionados laid out a course that wound along two-lane asphalt roads.

What followed was six years of racing by ever more-potent sports racing cars, including Cadillac-Allards and Jaguars, topped by Porsche Spyders, Ferraris and Bill Stroppe's Kurtis 500S. Safety on the 2.4-mile course was a problem as cars sped through the coastal forest without benefit of guardrails.

The end came in April 1956 when in the main event Ernie McAfee lost control of his Ferrari, hit a tree and was killed. Racing was moved inland to Laguna Seca Raceway, a closed course. All that remains is the International Concours at the Pebble Beach Country Club.

Photo: Michael Lynch
Map: at right - 1951; at left - 1968

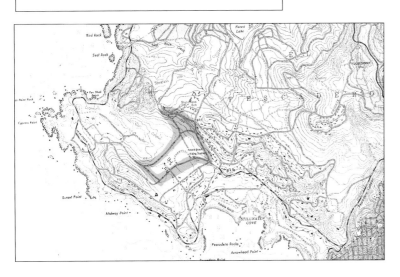

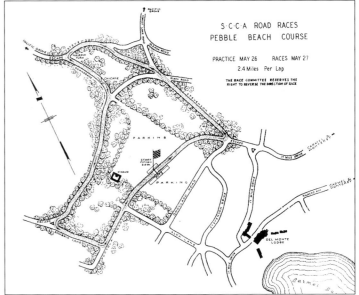

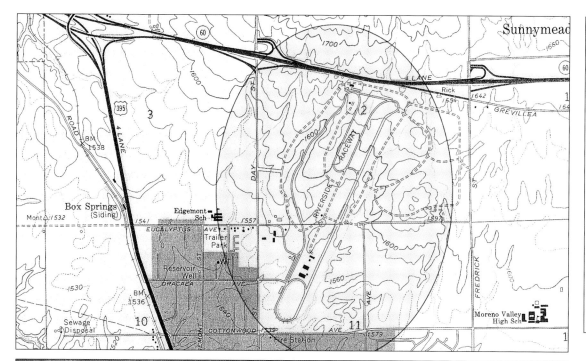

Riverside International Raceway, California

Riverside Raceway, about 60 miles south of Los Angeles at the junction of I-215 and Route 60, with a paved oval, a drag strip and road courses up to 3.275 miles long, opened in 1957. Ritchie Ginther won the first race, for sports cars. In the photograph Dan Gurney and Carroll Shelby dice in turn six on April 3, 1960. USAC, CART, IMSA, NASCAR and other kinds of racing competed there until 1988, when the real estate became worth more than the racing income could support. NASCAR legend Joe Weatherly was killed there in 1964.

Photo: Bob Tronolone

Map: 1967

Santa Monica, California

In 1909 the Los Angeles Automobile Dealers Association sought to capitalize on what had become in the east a thriving business of auto racing on public roads. They laid out an 8.4-mile course in nearby Santa Monica, starting on Ocean Avenue at Montana, a curving "D" shaped course on streets that exist today.

Harris Hanshue, in an Apperson Jackrabbit, won the first large car race on July 10, 1909. In 1914 Santa Monica attracted the ninth running of the Vanderbilt Cup races in which John Maquis took this spill in a Sunbeam at "Death Corner"—Ocean Avenue and Wilshire. Ralph DePalma won that race in a Mercedes. Dario Resta in a Peugeot was the victor in the 1916 Cup contest. The final race was run on March 15, 1919. By then lap speeds were nearing 100 mph, too fast for safety on city streets, and the Santa Monica road races came to an end.

Photo: Smithsonian

Map: 1914

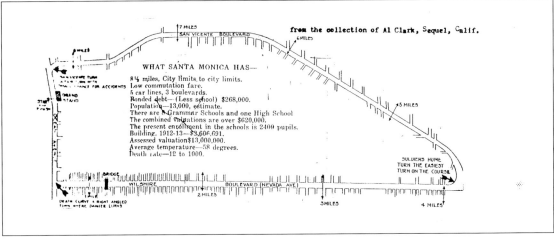

from the collection of Al Clark, Sequel, Calif.

WHAT SANTA MONICA HAS—

8¼ miles, City limits, to city limits.
Low commutation fare.
5 car lines, 3 boulevards.
Bonded debt— (Less school) $268,000.
Population—13,000, estimate.
There are 8 Grammar Schools and one High School
The combined valuations are over $620,000.
The present enrollment in the schools is 2400 pupils.
Building, 1912-13—$3,606,691.
Assessed valuation $13,000,000.
Average temperature—58 degrees.
Death rate—12 to 1000.

Lakeside Speedway, Denver, Colorado

Lakeside Amusement Park, at West 45th and Sheridan Boulevard in Denver, was built in 1935 by Ben Krasner. Three years later he turned the park's baseball field into a 1/5-mile track for the midgets, which were at the time attracting large crowds. Lloyd Axel won the first race on April 24, 1938. A year later the track was paved and Roy Sherman won the first race on asphalt.

Lakeside was a top midget track for many years and Axel continued to dominate the winner's circle. When the midgets began to fade in 1950, Krasner brought in stock cars, though the midgets raced there as well for many years. After Krasner died his daughter operated the track until 1988 when economics and the death of a spectator finally brought racing at Lakeside to an end. The track itself still exists today as a parking lot.

Photo: LeRoy Byers

Map: 1957

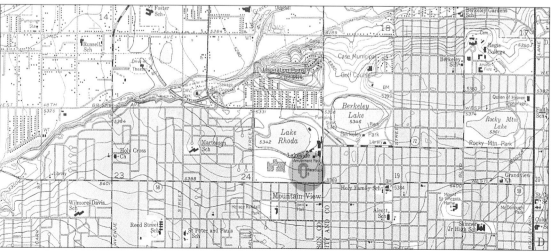

Danbury, Connecticut

The Danbury Fairgrounds were built in 1908 on Backus Avenue next to the airport about two miles southwest of Danbury. At first the fairgrounds had a 1/2-mile dirt oval where "big cars" ran. In 1940 a 1/5-mile track was added for the midgets. After World War II it was expanded to 1/4-mile and paved in 1958. The midget track had a shallow boat-racing lagoon next to it where more than one racing car took an unplanned bath. The track closed in 1981 and in the early 1990s the site became a shopping center. In the photograph a field of big cars race into the first turn in a 1939 event.

Photo: Joseph Freeman

Map: 1972

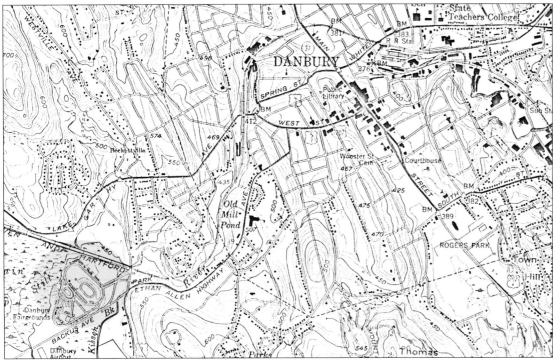

Daytona Beach, Florida

The hard, firm sand of Ormond and Daytona beaches became a place to test fast cars beginning in 1908 and the beach saw runs by the world's greatest cars and drivers for 30 years. Sig Haugdahl went 180 mph there in 1923 and Frank Lockhart crashed to his death on the sands in 1928. In 1936 the AAA sanctioned a 3.6-mile stock car race at Daytona Beach Shores that Milt Marion won in a new Ford roadster. Beginning in 1947 NASCAR held Speedweek runs on the beach and in 1948 began twelve years of Grand National racing on a 4.1-mile course at what is now Ponce Inlet. The cars raced north on the beach to the present Sun Dunes Circle then turned south on to Atlantic Avenue (Highway A1A) to Ocean Way Drive. In 1960 NASCAR moved the race from the beach to the present Daytona International Speedway.

Photo: IMHF

Map: 1956

Grandstands

Miami-Fulford Speedway, Fulford, Florida

The Miami-Fulford Board Speedway, with turns banked 50 degrees, had the briefest of lives and saw one race, on February 22, 1926, won by Peter DePaolo in the Duesenberg in which he had won the 1925 Indianapolis 500. Eight months after the track was built and before another race could be run the great hurricane of September 1926 turned the wooden track into acres of kindling.

The site, called Fulford-by-the-Sea in 1926, is now in North Miami Beach. The track was located east of I-95, west of NE 18th Avenue and north of NE 191st Street, on land that became the Diplomat Presidential Golf Course. On the ground the outline of the track survived into the 1950s.

Photos: Joseph Freeman

Map: 1950

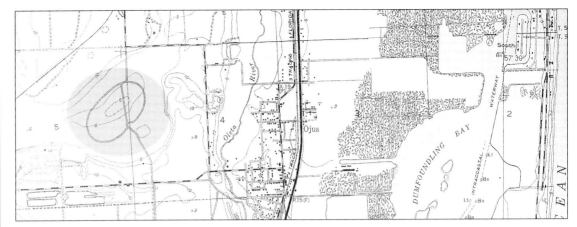

Plant Field, Tampa, Florida

Plant Field, named for Henry Plant, founder of University of Tampa, was built in 1921 on North Brevard Street at what is now John F. Kennedy Boulevard in downtown Tampa and was used as the South Florida State Fairgrounds. Alex Sloan was the first auto racing promoter and he ran International Motor Contest Association big car events on the 1/2-mile dirt track in the late winter and early spring before the racers moved north for the summer season. Charlie Roe is seen here winning the first recorded race.

After Sloan died, Dick Edwards ran IMCA sprinters and stocks until 1980 when the University converted the fairgrounds into an athletic field. The track was finally demolished in May, 2002.

Photo: Bruce Craig

Map: 1956

Atlanta Motordrome, Georgia

Asa G. Candler, the druggist who became a multi-millionaire by inventing Coca-Cola, built a two-mile, $400,000 clay track designed to be "the Indianapolis of the South" on Virginia Avenue at Atlanta Avenue, in Hapeville, south of Atlanta, in 1909. Louis Chevrolet won the first race, and the Coca-Cola trophy, on November 9 during the annual Atlanta Automobile Show. It was an immense success. Succeeding races featured Barney Oldfield, Louis Strang and similar stars.

In 1910 an air show was added, starring pilot Eugene B. Ely, who lost a race to E.M.F. auto driver Harry Cohen. However, race receipts were too poor to support the track. Ray Harroun, who would later win the first Indianapolis 500, won the final race on October 6.

The track lay dormant for 19 years, with early aviators using a part of the infield as a flying field. In 1927, spurred by the Lindbergh flight, Atlanta bought the land as its municipal airport, Candler Field. Candler became Hartsfield International. The last visible banking of the racetrack was bulldozed away in 1970 because it interfered with the tower's visibility of a taxiway.

Photo: Philip Harms
Map: 1954

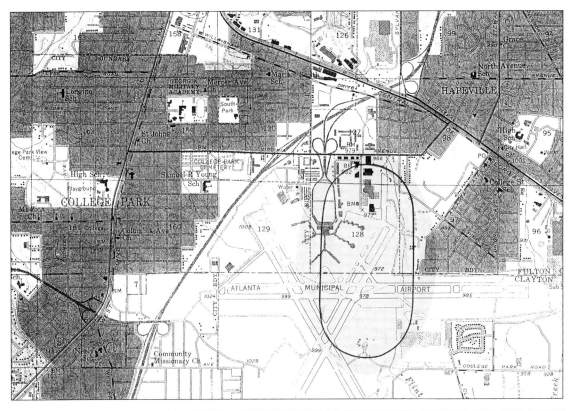

28

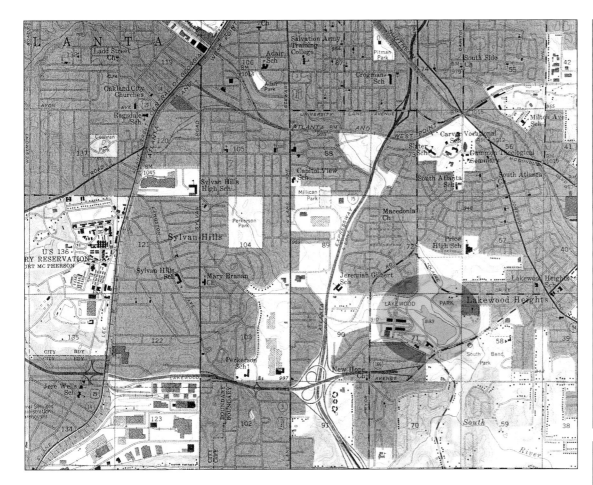

Lakewood, Georgia

The Southeastern Fairgrounds were built in 1915 at Lakewood Park, on Poole's Creek Reservoir, Atlanta's first waterworks. Exhibition buildings were erected and Grand Circuit horse races were held on the 1-mile track encircling the lake. In 1917 motorcycle races began and Ralph DePalma ran match races in his Packard against Barney Oldfield in the Miller Golden Submarine. During the 1920s and 1930s the fairgrounds track was fought over by big cars from IMCA and the AAA. CSRA stock car racing began in 1938.

George Robson was killed at Lakewood, three months after he won the 1946 Indianapolis 500, and Frank Luptow died there in 1952. Eventually competition from the Six Flags amusement park and Road Atlanta killed both the fairs and the racing at Lakewood which came to an end in 1979.

Photo: Mike Bell

Map: 1968

Boise Fairgrounds, Idaho

The Idaho Intermountain Fair Association built a 1/2-mile dirt racetrack at Fairview Avenue and Orchard Street in Boise in 1897. In 1910 Barney Oldfield came to town and set a new world's record there with his big Knox. In 1915 Barney was back with the front-drive Christie and DeLloyd Thompson in a biplane on a swing through the West that included Montana, Utah and Nevada. Thompson was billed as "The World's Greatest Aviator" and, of course, Barney was "The Master Driver of the World." Thompson won the car versus plane race by a whisker.

The photograph shows a Boise race in 1922. The track was subsequently re-named the Western Idaho State Fairgrounds. When I-84 was built in the 1960s the fair moved to Glenwood Street and the old site was cleared for the construction of a mini-mall.

Photo: Don Radbruch

Map: 1954

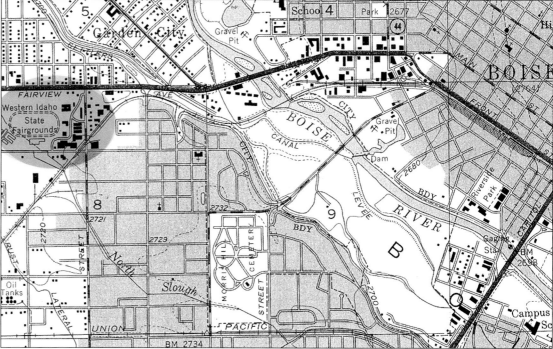

Chicago Speedway Park, Maywood, Illinois

In 1914 local promoters decided that Chicago needed a racetrack to rival Indianapolis. In April 1915 lumber magnate Edward J. Hines began construction of a 2-mile wooden oval next to the Aviation Field at Maywood, about ten miles west of the Loop. Dario Resta, in a Peugeot, won the first race and a $23,000 purse on June 26, 1915 before 85,000 fans. Unfortunately for the owners, World War I diverted attention from auto racing. Bad management led to a downward spiral of too many races too close together before too few spectators. The final event ended ignominiously in the rain on July 28, 1918. Hines' son was killed in the trenches in France and his father used steel from the grandstands to build a hospital as a memorial to him. Hines subsequently sold the hospital to the Federal Government's Veterans Bureau and it was still a VA hospital in 2002. (Also seen on this map is the outline of the Harlem 1-mile dirt track of 1905 to 1907.)

Photo: Philip Harms

Diagram: Author's Collection

Map: 1928

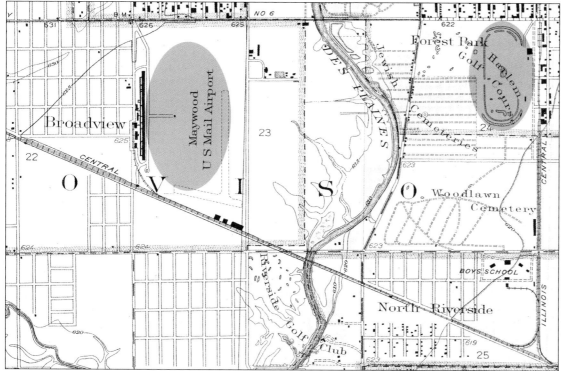

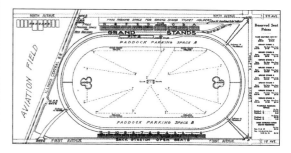

Elgin Road Races, Elgin, Illinois

In 1910 Frank Wood of Elgin, Illinois persuaded the Chicago Motor Club to hold a 305-mile road race in his town, about 40 miles northwest of Chicago. The course wound 8.36 miles over bumpy Kane County macadam roads. Cleverly, the organizers pacified the local farmers by sharing the proceeds with them. From the start the competitors drove west along Highland Avenue, south on Randall Road to U.S. Route 20, east on Larkin Avenue to McLean and back to Highland. The Elgin Watch Company provided a beautiful 44-inch tall silver Tiffany's trophy to Ralph Mulford, the winner, and watches for all of the drivers.

The races continued each August until 1915 when World War I halted the contest. They were resumed in 1919 only to fail financially in 1920. The Elgin races were revived in 1933 under AAA sanction and two races were held; one for Indianapolis cars and the other for stock Ford and Plymouth roadsters. Fred Frame won the stock car race while Phil Shafer in a Buick won the Indy Car event.

Photo: Joseph Freeman

Map: 1952

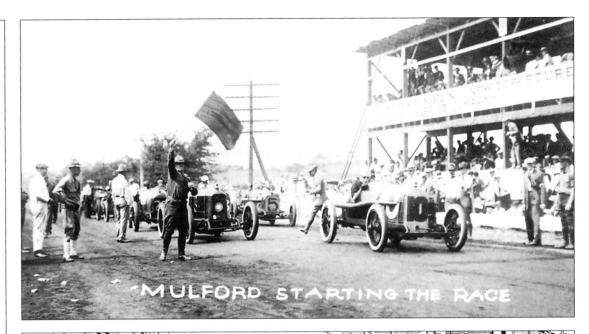

MULFORD STARTING THE RACE

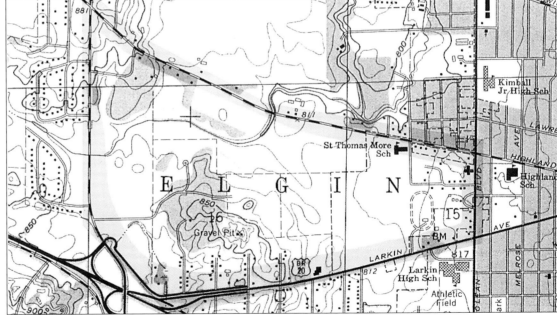

Soldier Field, Chicago, Illinois

Built in classical style in 1924 as Grant Park Municipal Stadium, Soldier Field was re-named in 1925. Intended as a multi-purpose facility, a 1/4-mile dirt racetrack was installed in 1935. Over the next 33 years a board track and paved tracks of 3/8- and 1/2-mile were used there at different times. Soldier Field saw midgets, stock cars (seen here in 1952), Andy Granatelli's Hurricane Hot Rod Association and NASCAR Grand National cars drawing crowds that reached nearly 70,000. The end came when the Chicago Bears football team moved in and the racetrack was removed to allow more seating for NFL football games.

Photo: Bob Sheldon

Map: 1939

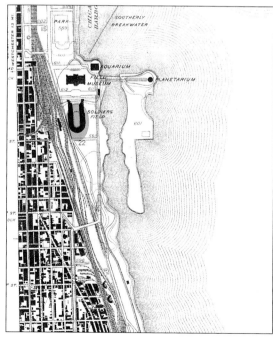

Times-Herald Race, Chicago, Illinois

The first scheduled auto race in America was held on Thanksgiving Day, November 28, 1895, along a 52.4-mile course over city streets from Jackson Park, site of the 1893 World's Fair, north to Evanston, and back to the starting line via Garfield Park. Deep snow that had fallen the night before made the route treacherous. Only two of the six cars entered actually finished the race; the victorious American Duryea, in 10 hours 23 minutes and the second place Benz, in 10 hours 53 minutes. (Because of an error by judges along the route the Benz actually ran a slightly shorter distance.) Duryea spent 55 minutes at a blacksmith shop forging a new steering arm after his broke. Seen here, Duryea leads Jerry O'Connor in the Macy-Benz while passing through Evanston.

Photo: Times-Herald

Drawing: Smithsonian (opposite page)

Map: 1945

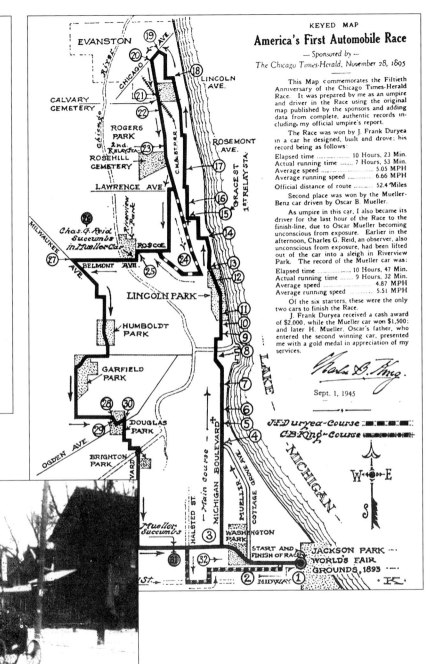

KEYED MAP

America's First Automobile Race

— Sponsored by —
The Chicago Times-Herald, November 28, 1895

This Map commemorates the Fiftieth Anniversary of the Chicago Times-Herald Race. It was prepared by me as an umpire and driver in the Race using the original map published by the sponsors and adding data from complete, authentic records including, my official umpire's report.

The Race was won by J. Frank Duryea in a car he designed, built and drove; his record being as follows:

Elapsed time .... 10 Hours, 23 Min.
Actual running time .... 7 Hours, 53 Min.
Average speed .... 5.05 MPH
Average running speed .... 6.66 MPH
Official distance of route .... 52.4 Miles

Second place was won by the Mueller-Benz car driven by Oscar B. Mueller.

As umpire in this car, I also became its driver for the last hour of the Race to the finish-line, due to Oscar Mueller becoming unconscious from exposure. Earlier in the afternoon, Charles G. Reid, an observer, also unconscious from exposure, had been lifted out of the car into a sleigh in Riverview Park. The record of the Mueller car was:

Elapsed time .... 10 Hours, 47 Min.
Actual running time .... 9 Hours, 32 Min.
Average speed .... 4.87 MPH
Average running speed .... 5.51 MPH

Of the six starters, these were the only two cars to finish the Race.

J. Frank Duryea received a cash award of $2,000, while the Mueller car won $1,500; and later H. Mueller, Oscar's father, who entered the second winning car, presented me with a gold medal in appreciation of my services.

Charles B. King

Sept. 1, 1945

J.F.Duryea-Course ▪▪▪▪▪
C.B.King-Course ▪▪▪▪▪

Fort Wayne Speedway, Indiana

The Allen County Fairgrounds north of Fort Wayne on Coliseum Road at Northrup Street was a 5/8-mile high-banked dirt track where racing began in about 1928. Frank Funk paved the track in 1937 and a dirt 1/2-mile oval was laid out inside the larger track, then after World War II a paved 1/4-mile midget track was built inside the half. In CSRA big car races at Fort Wayne Rex Woodward was killed in Al Singer's Voelker while Sid Bufkin died in the crash of the Wilson Ranger. Bob Chilcote died in a stock car crash at Fort Wayne in 1953.

The track was torn down in 1965 and new fairgrounds were built further north on Carroll Road. The old track site was sold to the Ford Motor Company. In the photograph here from the 1940s Duke Nalon in the Vance No. 2 has the pole while Pappy Booker in the Jewel Hal No. 34 rides the outside.

Photo: Bob McConnell

Map: 1963

Jungle Park Speedway, Jungle Park, Indiana

The remains of Jungle Park Speedway still lie at Turkey Run along US Route 41, nine miles north of Rockville, Indiana. The track has been silent since 1963. Built by Earl Padgett in 1920, Jungle Park was a shapeless, wobbly circle, un-fenced, over a part dirt, part paved, part banked surface. A 1/4-mile dirt midget track was added in the 1940s. Frank Funk, the famed Midwest promoter, ran the track for a time. Many of the races at Jungle Park were open competition or were sanctioned by the independent MDTRA club.

Bobby Grim is one of the noted drivers who started his career there. The track closed after a spectator was killed by an out of control race car. In the photograph, a field of MDTRA cars get the green flag for a start with the pole car already out of shape.

Photo: Bob McConnell

Map: 1961

Roby Speedway, Hammond, Indiana

Roby Speedway, also known as Lakeside, was a 1-mile oiled dirt oval built in Hammond, Indiana in 1920, a few feet from the Illinois State line at Indianapolis Boulevard and 107th Street. I-90, the Dan Ryan Expressway, runs through the site today.

Driver Billy Arnold began his career at Roby and B. Ward Beam was an early promoter. The track ran an early version of stock car races in the twenties, but was better known for "big car" competition in the 1930s. The track closed after a driver fatality in 1936 followed by a car going into the grandstands and injuring several spectators.

Photo: Bob Sheldon

Map: 1937

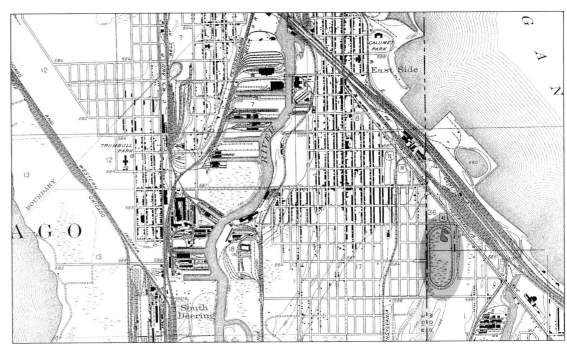

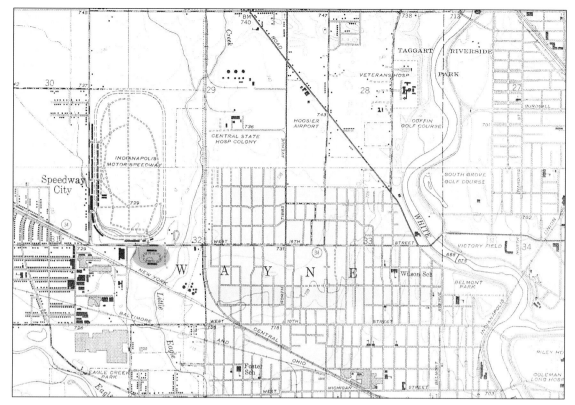

West 16th Street - Indianapolis Midget Speedway, Indianapolis, Indiana

In 1946, with the midgets in their post-World War II boom, promoter Rags Mitchell built a 1/4-mile paved oval across West 16th Street from the Indianapolis Motor Speedway. It became one of the premier midget tracks in the country, especially in the month of May when all the hot shoes in the nation were in town either looking for a ride at the Speedway or just enjoying the camaraderie. The night before the 500 Mitchell would run three complete programs in the afternoon, at dusk and at midnight. The property was sold to make way for a shopping center in 1959.

Below is a picture of Bob Harmer watching Johnny Kay get into the DiHiCo Offy in 1956.

Photos: Bruce Craig

Map: 1948

Sioux City Speedway, Iowa

Promoters built a 2-mile dirt track six miles northwest of Sioux City (actually in Stevens, South Dakota) in 1914 where AAA championship races were run in 1914 and 1915. Eddie Rickenbacker won both the 1914 and 1915 contests in a Duesenberg. Dario Resta put so much wear and tear on his Peugeot in the July 3, 1915, race that he was unable to run at the opening race on the nearby Omaha board track two days later.

The last race was held July 4, 1917, and the grandstands were torn down during the first World War.

The site was later turned into Rickenbacker Airfield.

Photo: Joe Freeman

Map: 1914

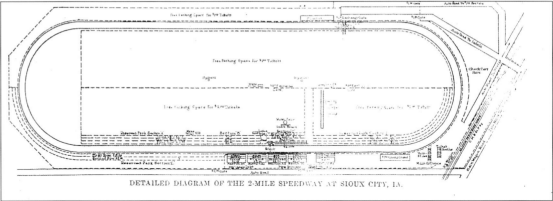

DETAILED DIAGRAM OF THE 2-MILE SPEEDWAY AT SIOUX CITY, IA.

RALPH HEPBURN ON HARLEY-DAVIDSON EIGHT VALVE MACHINE WHICH EXCEEDED 100, 200 AND 300 MILE WORLD RECORDS AT DODGE CITY, KANSAS, JULY 4, 1921.

Dodge City Speedway, Kansas

There have been two tracks at Dodge City, Kansas that have faded into history. The largest was the 2-mile track built in 1913 by J. P. McCollom for motorcycle racing by the Kansas Short Grass Motorcycle Club. Built in a field northeast of Comanche Street and Avenue P, it was used for the 300-mile "Coyote Classic" on July 4, 1913, with Glenn "Slivers" Boyd the winner on an 8-valve Indian. Local papers called the track "the best dirt track in the world." In 1915, before a crowd of 17,000, Otto Walker won and in 1916 Irving Janke edged out Floyd Clymer for the victory at what had become the Indianapolis of motorcycle racing.

Clymer became publisher of the Indianapolis 500 yearbook in 1946 and Ralph Hepburn, who ran away with the 1921 Dodge City motorcycle classic, turned to the driving of Indianapolis cars in 1925.

In the early 1930s a 1/2-mile dirt track was built at Wright Park, on Park Street at 2nd Avenue, known most familiarly as McCarty Speedway. It was a stop on the IMCA big car circuit in the 1930s. Clymer was the promoter in the 1960s and there was motorcycle racing at McCarty through the late 1990s until it was replaced by a new Dodge City Raceway Park at US Route 283 and 14th Avenue.

Photo: Ford County Historical Society
Map: 1970

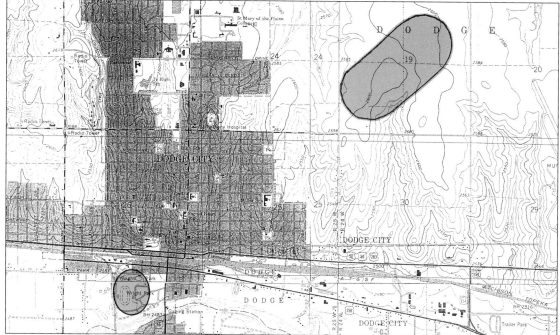

Louisiana State Fair track, Shreveport, Louisiana

The Louisiana State Fair track at Shreveport was built in 1870 as a 1-mile oval for horse racing. The Louisiana state fair opened there in 1906. The first recorded auto race was a 1910 appearance by Barney Oldfield. The covered grandstands went up in 1912. In 1913, J. Alex Sloan brought in Louis Disbrow and Wild Bill Endicott; later Sloan stars were Fred Horey, then Jules Ellingboe in the Golden Submarine. In 1938 the track was shortened to a 1/2-mile while Sloan continued as the promoter under IMCA, with stars as Gus Schrader, Emory Collins, Ben Shaw, Ben Musick, Buddy Calloway, Dave Champeau and Jimmy Wilburn. Schrader was killed there in an odd Wednesday race, October 22, 1941.

A 1/4-mile track added in the infield after World War II was not a success. The IMCA promoted big cars, midgets (IMCA called them "compact sprint cars"), and stock cars on the half-mile into the late 1960s. Paving the larger track in 1969 was not successful because the dirt cars could not compete on asphalt and they lost the star IMCA drivers.

The final event was the Louisiana State Stock Car Championship in 1977. The track was torn up in 1981 and the grandstands demolished in 1984. In the photograph the IMCA stock cars open the 1958 season in the Pelican 300 with Don White on the pole in 1957 Ford No. 1.

Photo: Ernie Roberson

Map: 1955

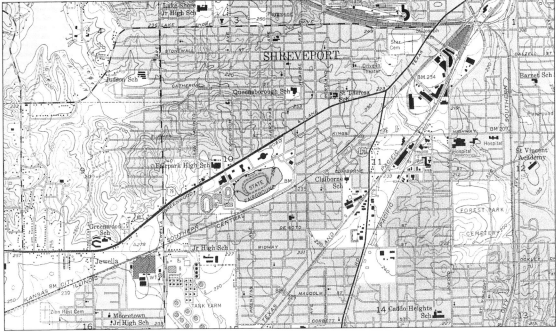

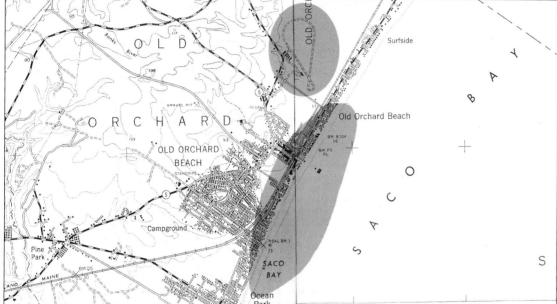

Old Orchard Beach, Maine

There were two racecourses at Old Orchard Beach, site of the amusement park just south of Portland. For two years the Maine sands rivaled Ormond Beach. Beginning September 4, 1911, drivers from the J. Alex Sloan stable including Louis Disbrow, Harry Endicott, Harry Cobe and John Rutherford ran on the beach itself, Rutherford setting a lap record of 99.66 mph before the tide came in and halted the event. In AAA races in July 1912 Disbrow set a new record of 102.5 mph in the chain-drive J-I-C Fiat. Participants included Harry Grant, Dave Lewis, Joe Nikrent and Joe Matson, some of whom had run at Indianapolis. "Outlaw" beach races continued until 1916.

The second track was across the railroad tracks from the beach. A mile and an eighth long, it was shaped like a figure "8" (although drivers did not cross the loop). The track operated from about 1928 until just before World War II.

Photos: Joseph Freeman

Map: 1944

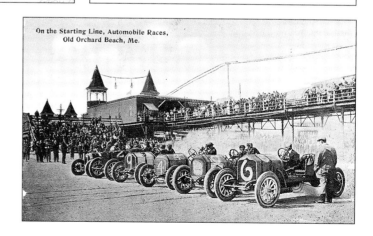

43

Marlboro Motor Raceway, Marlboro, Maryland

Marlboro Motor Raceway, 19 miles southeast of Washington, D.C., was built originally as a 1/3-mile dirt oval in 1952. Reds Fowler was killed there in 1953 in a stock car. The track was paved in 1954 and a year later a sports car group known as the "Lavender Hill Mob" hustled the money to add a 1.7-mile road course. It was one of two sports car tracks in the country to run counter-clockwise. Over 17 years it saw sprints, midgets and stock cars, but it was best known for SCCA sports car racing. Trans-Am races were run there in 1966 and 1967, with Bob Tulius and Tony Adamowicz the winners of the 1966 12-hour event in a Dodge Dart and Jerry Titus and Bert Everett took the 1967 300 miler in a Porsche 911.

During the 1960s the track ran a "Refrigerator Bowl" race each winter, usually a "run whatcha brung" event that mixed midgets, sports cars and stock cars. In the photograph Elmo Langley in the No. 66 Rastus Walters Grand National Ford is starting the race with open-wheel formula cars.

The track closed in 1969 because of a number of problems after Summit Point opened in West Virginia and the SCCA moved there. The course and part of the stands could still be seen in 2002.

Photo: Venlo Wolfsohn

Map: 1957

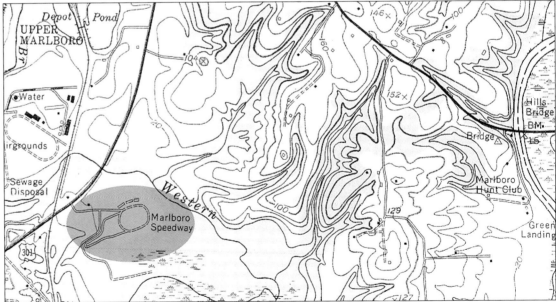

Boston Gardens, Massachusetts

Boston Gardens, an indoor arena, was built in 1928 on Causeway Street, over North Station. The home of the Boston Bruins hockey team and the Celtics basketball team, it played host to midget racing for three years beginning in 1936. There was initially a 1/10-mile dirt oval in the Gardens but later the cars ran on the flat wooden floor. Bill Schindler won the opening race. A banked wood track was built in sections outside, disassembled and set up indoors late in 1937. The midgets ran there in the winter of 1937 and part of 1938. The photo shows the cars lined up in the "pits" in the infield before the races in February, 1937.

The Gardens remained as a hockey and basketball arena until it was torn down in 1995. The site is now the Fleet Center and a federal building.

Photo: Joseph Freeman
Map: 1980

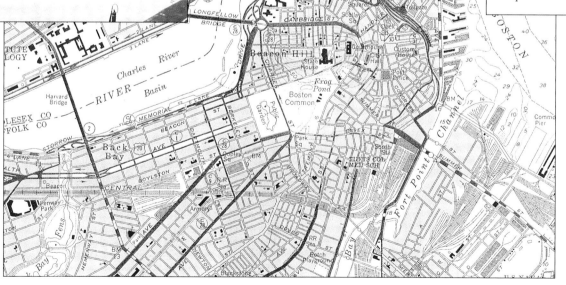

Brockton Fairgrounds, Massachusetts

The Brockton Fairgrounds were located at Forest Avenue and Belmont Street, west of town. The 1/2-mile dirt oval was first used for auto racing in 1920, with an AAA sanction in 1927. According to local legend, 54,000 fans crowded into the grounds for one 1934 AAA big car event. Seen here is the start of the "Governor Curley Sweepstakes," September 18, 1935. The original grandstands were destroyed by fire in 1936, but were eventually rebuilt. In 1938 Ben Shaw won an IMCA race at Brockton over Gus Schrader before 30,000 spectators. A 1/4-mile track was scraped out of the infield in 1940 for the midgets. The fairgrounds were demolished in 1973.

Photo: Joseph Freeman

Map: 1949

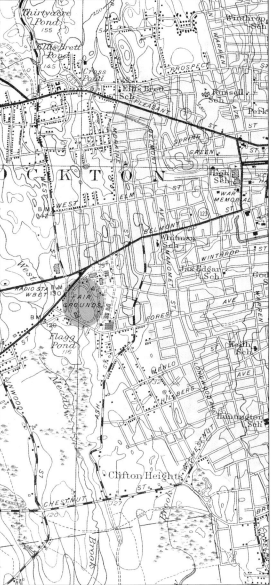

Lowell, Massachusetts

Lowell had a famous road race, first run on Labor Day 1908, for 24 laps over a 10.6-mile route dubbed "The Merrimack Valley Road Course." It ran west on a stretch of Pawtucket Boulevard known as the "speedway" to Tyngsboro Bridge, then back on Sherburne and Varnum Avenues to Dunbar Street and thence back to Pawtucket. Louis Strang was the victor, averaging 54 miles an hour in a 600 cubic inch Isotta-Fraschini. The race was one of the first to be sanctioned by the just-established Contest Board of the American Automobile Association.

A year later the Butler Ames Silver Cup and two other trophies were offered, plus prizes for straight-away speed trials on the "speedway." Barney Oldfield, in the Blitzen Benz, took the flying mile at more than 90 miles per hour to capture the straightaway prize.

In the 318 mile feature race, seen here, Burt Shaw (in the No. 15 Stoddard-Dayton) leads the No. 16 Apperson past the start-finish line. George Robertson won the event in a Simplex averaging 51 miles per hour.

Though the races at Lowell were sporting successes they lost money for the town and upset some citizens who did not appreciate having the public roads used for competition. The 1909 Lowell Road Race was the last of the major races there, though legend has it that there was a smaller event in 1912.

Photo: Joseph Freeman
Map: 1965

Norwood Arena, Norwood, Massachusetts

The Norwood Arena was one of the New England short tracks that sprang up in 1948 during the heyday of the midgets; a paved 1/4-mile oval, it was built on the site of an abandoned sewage disposal plant about five miles south of Readville. Rain postponed opening day twice, but Johnny Bernardi won the inaugural race on June 14, 1948 in a Kurtis Offy midget. Norwood opened just as the midget craze was winding down, so shortly it began to run the cheaper slam-bang late-model stock cars. Seen here is the start of a 24-hour stock car enduro on April 18, 1949. A drag strip was added in 1960. Dave Dion in a late model was the track's last champion in 1972. The site, at Ridge River Drive east of US Route 1 is now an industrial park.

Photo: Tommy Caruso

Map: 1970

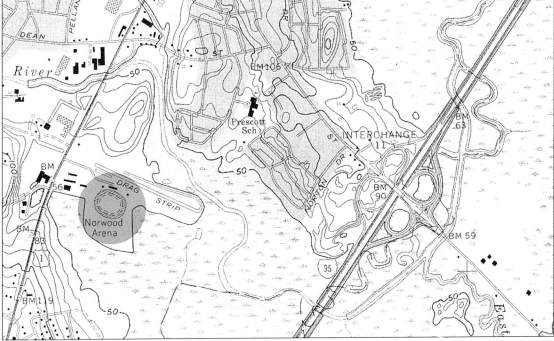

Readville, Massachusetts

A 1-mile dirt track for trotting races was built on the west shore of the Neponset River on the present Meadow Street in Hyde Park, Massachusetts, in about 1900. The first recorded auto race there was in 1902 and, shown in the photograph, Ralph DePalma won his first race ever at a Readville contest in 1908. There may have been IMCA races in 1915, but the AAA sanctioned one race in 1924 that attracted Jimmy Murphy, Peter DePaolo and Bennie Hill. Independent groups such as Dick Dunn's New England Auto Racing Association also sanctioned races such as those on the 4th of July and Labor Day, 1934. The ARCA sports cars ran at Readville on May 30, 1935. A six-car pileup in a roadster race in 1933 trapped driver Al Fraser of Haverford, Pennsylvania, who burned to death. Three years later in the mid-summer of 1936 Wes Johnson, of Lansdown, Pennsylvania died and Rex Mays was seriously injured in a crash caused by dust that obscured the track. Following that accident the AAA insisted that the track be oiled with "asphalt emulsion" to reduce the dust before they would allow the 1936 Labor day races to be held.

The hurricane of 1938 severely damaged the grandstands and washed out part of the track, bringing an end to racing at Readville. The site was used by the Air Corps as an emergency landing strip during World War II and is now occupied by a grocery warehouse.

Photo: Joseph Freeman
Map: 1946

49

Detroit Driving Park, Grosse Point, Michigan

Detroit Driving Club at Jefferson and Connors Avenues was a 1-mile dirt track built in 1893 to allow gentlemen drivers of the new-fangled automobile to exercise their cars. Banked turns were expected to allow the then considered blinding speed of "a mile a minute." In 1901 Daniel Campeau, manager of the Driving Club and Charles Shanks, the sales manager of the Alexander Winton Company of Cleveland, cooked up a series of races in order to show the Winton Automobile's superiority. The 70 horsepower Winton was expected to be an easy winner over all comers.

Henry Ford challenged Winton with his lighter 26 horsepower vehicle. On race day, October 10, 1901, Winton took an early lead against the inexperienced Ford in the 10-lap affair. Henry plucked up his nerve and began to gain on Winton, finally passing him with two laps to go, as shown here. Ford never drove in another race, one was enough. Grosse Pointe was the race that made Ford a household name. A year later Barney Oldfield again defeated Winton at Grosse Point driving Ford's next racing car, the "999."

The track survived until 1915 when a Hudson assembly plant was built on the site. Today both are gone and Kitchener and Navahoe Streets, lined with expensive residences, occupy the site.

Photo: Smithsonian
Map: 1905

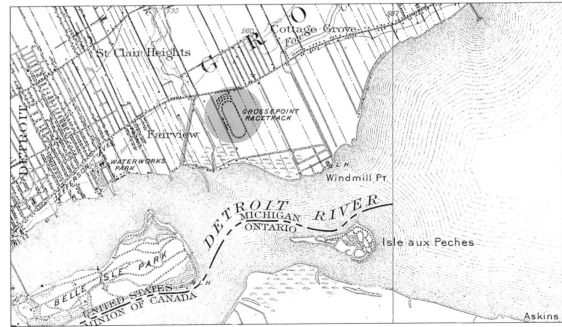

50

Motor City Speedway, Detroit, Michigan

Don and Carson Zeiter built a 1/2-mile oiled dirt oval at Eight Mile Road and Schoenherr Road in 1932 and cut it down to a 1/4-mile midget track in 1936. Over the years the track was known variously as VFW Speedway, Motor City Speedway, New Detroit Speedway and simply as Zeiters. It saw big cars, midgets, sprint cars, championship cars, stock cars and roadsters race. The last races were run there in 1958 and the site is now a shopping center.

Upper photo: Jim O'Keefe

Lower photo: Allan Brown

Map: 1941

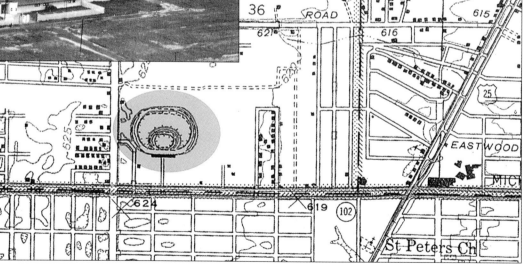

Packard Proving Grounds, Utica, Michigan

The Packard Motor Company built a concrete oval, 2 1/2-miles in circumference, in Utica, Michigan in 1928 as part of its test and proving grounds. The track was used for at least one exhibition race and that same year Leon Duray, seen here, drove his supercharged Miller 91 front-drive Indianapolis car 148.17 miles an hour, faster than Frank Lockhart's incredible 147 mph qualifying lap at Atlantic City in 1927.

The track, located between 22 and 23 Mile roads and Van Dyke and Mound, was bought by the Ford Motor Company after Packard's demise. It was to have been turned into a U.S. Mail postal facility, but the deal fell through. The track may soon be truncated at its northern end to widen 23 Mile Road.

Photo: EMMR

Map: 1983

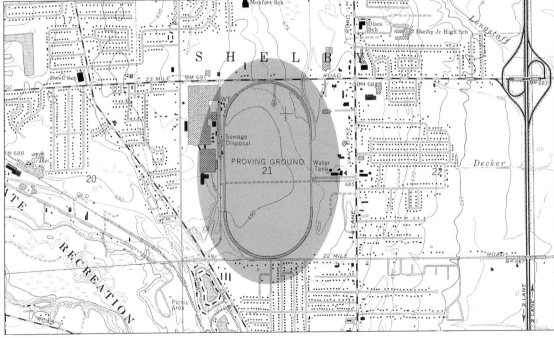

Twin Cities Motor Speedway, Fort Snelling, Minnesota

Twin Cities Motor Speedway was first planned to be built in 1913 on a tract north of St. Paul, but before construction started it was shifted to a larger open area a mile and a half west of Fort Snelling, an Indian Wars fort built in 1819. The 2-mile concrete track was finished in 1915 at a cost of $900,000, using 40,000 barrels of cement. Earl Cooper, in a Stutz, won the first race, a 500-mile AAA-sanctioned affair on Labor Day, 1915.

Ralph DePalma took the July 4, 1916, 150-miler in his Mercedes, and Ira Vail won a July 17, 1917, event, the last race to be held there.

After the track fell into disuse, the Twin City Aero Club began to use the flat area in the infield as a landing area, as the photograph shows. In 1921 Speedway Field was re-named Wold-Chamberlin after two local World War I pilots. It has developed into Minneapolis and St. Paul's International Airport.

Photo: Metro Airports Commission

Map: 1920

Diagram: EMMR

Kansas City Speedway, Kansas City, Missouri

Jack Prince and Art Pillsbury spent $500,000 of their investors' cash in 1922 building a 1 1/4-mile board track just north of the present Bannister Road on the west bank of the Blue River. So swampy was the site that Pillsbury had to drive long pilings that never reached bedrock, allowing the finished track to sway slightly. Tommy Milton won the rain-delayed 300-mile opener in a Miller 183 after Roscoe Sarles crashed over the outside rail to his death.

There were two 250-mile races in 1923 under the new 122 cubic inch formula, plus the national motorcycle championships, but crowds never equaled the opening day numbers of 50,000. By 1924 the untreated wood was beginning to rot. The 4th of July event was trimmed to 150 miles because of the deterioration of the surface. The track was already in bankruptcy and, after Jimmy Murphy's victory, had seen its last race. The last event there was a locomotive crash staged by Will Pickens with two over-aged engines. It then lay derelict into the early 1930s until workmen were finally hired to clear away the remaining debris. During World War II Pratt & Whitney built an aircraft engine plant on the site.

Photo: Bill Rinke

Map: 1957

Diagram: Author's Collection

Poster: Will Pickens

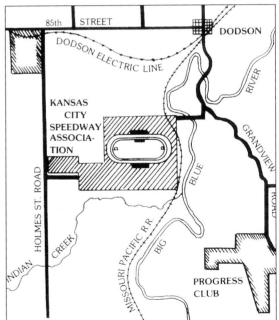

Olympic Stadium, Kansas City, Missouri

A 1/5-mile dirt oval was scraped out of the Blue River bottomlands in Independence in 1935 for Olympic Stadium and it became one of the most popular midget tracks in the Midwest. A. J. Foyt won his first USAC race there in May 1957. Jud Larson, Ben and Rabbit Musick and all of the Southwest hot shoes ran there during the midgets' best years. Bobby Marks was killed at Olympic in his brother's Ferguson Ford midget. Sammy Callahan was the starter there in the 1940s. The site is now a junkyard.

Photos: Bill Hill

Map: 1957

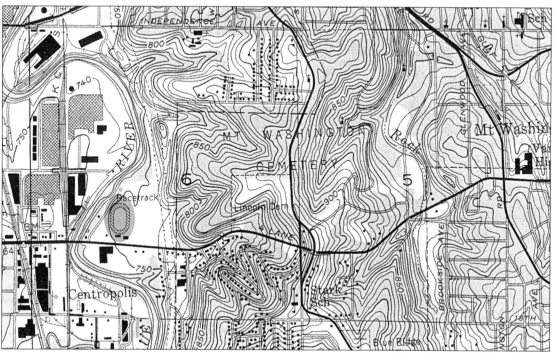

Lewis & Clark Fairgrounds, Helena, Montana

The Lewis & Clark Montana State Fairgrounds were built in 1870, with a 1-mile dirt track for horses. Barney Oldfield and DeLloyd Thompson came through Helena on a barnstorming tour in 1908 and the Case team raced there later. Recorded races were held at the fairgrounds in 1915 and 1924, almost certainly under IMCA sanction. Fairground officials cannot remember any auto races on their track in the past half-century. The fairgrounds only allow horses to run there today.

Photo: Don Radbruch

Map: 1985

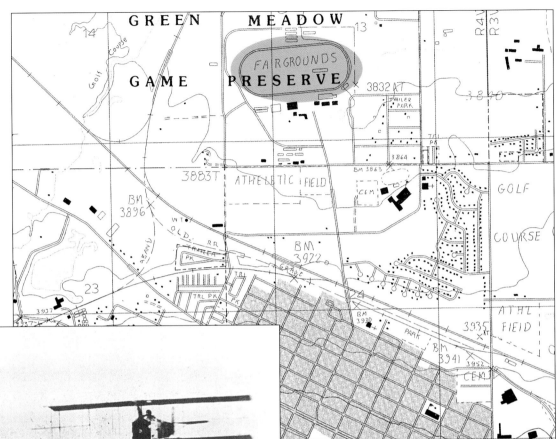

DeLloyd Thompson at Mont State Fair

Omaha Speedway, Ak-Sar-Ben Speedway, Omaha, Nebraska

Omaha had two tracks of note in days gone by, a board track that lasted but two years and a dirt track that survived for 84 years.

A successful contractor, Burt LeBron, built the Omaha board track, 1 1/4-miles in circumference, located at North Fifth Street and Hiatt Avenue near Carter Lake, in 1914. The first race, an AAA sanction, was held July 5, 1915, before 30,000 fans. The reigning star, Dario Resta, showed up, but his car was in such poor shape from the prior Sioux City race on July 3 that he could not run. Eddie Rickenbacker won the 300-miler in his Maxwell. In 1916 Resta and his Peugeot were ready and he took the July 15 150-mile race easily. Rickenbacker came back to win the 50-mile sprint with his Mercedes.

A year later the track's wood was in sad shape from the Nebraska weather. Ralph Mulford dodged holes in the boards to win the July Fourth 1917 race at an average of 102 miles per hour. Dave Lewis won a second, shorter race after emergency repairs were made to the track. It was the last turn of a wheel at Omaha's splinter palace.

About six miles to the west at 63rd Street and Woolworth another racetrack was doing much better. The 1-mile Omaha Speedway was built prior to 1910, originally as a horse track. The Ak-Sar-Ben Association (Nebraska spelled backwards) bought the site in 1919. Autos, from Barney Oldfield's onwards, raced at the track from 1910 until 1933 when the oat-burners got it back to themselves. Horse racing continued until 1994. The Kewitt Technical Center of the University of Nebraska now occupies the site and the last original building, a hockey rink, was due to be demolished in 2002.

Maps: Ak-Sar-Ben, 1956

  Omaha, 1915

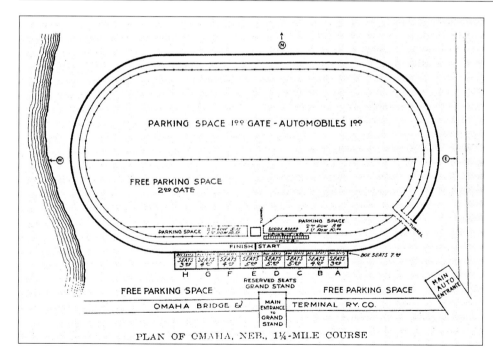

PLAN OF OMAHA, NEB., 1¼-MILE COURSE

Ord Fairgrounds, Nebraska

The Valley County Fair Association built the fairgrounds at Ord in 1926. Originally a 1/2-mile trotting track, attendance sagged and auto racing began with an AAA event in 1928. Slight banking on the turns was added in 1929. During the Depression most of the races were run as "independents," neither AAA nor IMCA sanctioned.

Ord was a town of only 5,000 but people would come for miles around to see the races. Sometimes crowds would exceed 10,000. One of Ord's problems was that the stands were on the north side of the track, the prevailing Nebraska winds were from the south, so the paying customers usually went home dusty. John Gerber won three races in August 1930 and when he took all three races the following year the rest of the drivers threatened to strike if Gerber was allowed to run at the next stop, Belleville, Kansas.

In 1938 the Fair Board cut a 1/4-mile midget track inside the big oval. On one race date in 1947 the fair ran big cars on the half in the afternoon and midgets at night on the quarter. Turns three and four of the larger track were plowed up in 1952, but the quarter lasted until 1965. The eastern end was sold and is now used for warehouses and a cattle sale operation. The Loup Valley Agricultural Society has an arena and holds 4-H and FFA events on what used to be turns one and two.

Photo: Roy Valasek

Map: 1954

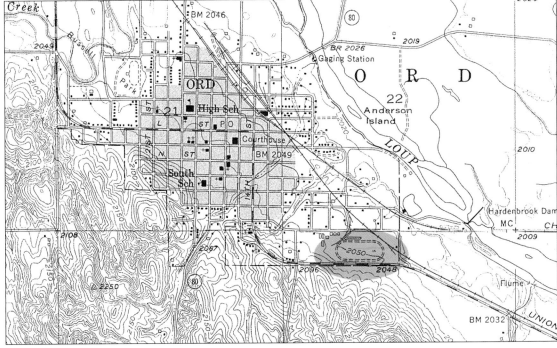

Lawton, Nevada

In 1937 a Nevada casino decided to spike up interest at their 1/4-mile dog track by running pari-mutuel midget races. There had been attempts in California, Maryland and New York to have betting on the midgets but authorities had quickly squelched them. Not so in Nevada, the casino operators thought.

The Springs Casino scheduled a weekend of racing at its dog track in Lawton Hot Springs east of Reno on the Truckee River and imported a field of California midget drivers including Paul Swedberg, Harry Alley, Duane Carter, Bob Barkheimer, Lloyd Logan and a few others.

In an attempt to keep the races honest (and protect the house from fixes) drivers were kept from talking to anyone after names were drawn for the lineup. The race schedule was set up, as are horse races, with eight races, the seventh being the feature and the eighth being a consolation.

According to Barkheimer, the competing casinos in Reno were unhappy at the new competition and "used their influence" to get the Nevada Highway Division to "repair" the road to the track, making it inconvenient to reach the races.

Photo: Joseph Freeman
Map: 1967

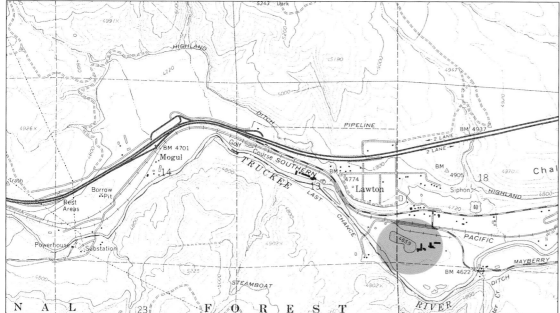

Bryar Motorsports Park, New Hampshire

Bryar was first built as a kart track in 1960. The next year a 1/5-mile oiled dirt oval was added where stock cars were raced briefly. The oval was paved in 1964-'65 when a 1.63-mile road course was added as a track upon which to run the Loudon Classic, when the Belknap Recreation Area booted the motorcycle racers out after an event in 1963 that ended in a near-riot.

In 1968 a 1/2-mile paved track was added to the infield of the road course and the next year a 1/3-mile dirt oval was put down inside the half. At this time Bryar was regularly running Trans-Am and other high-profile sports car and motorcycle events as well as NASCAR late model races. Mud bog and scrambles courses were built along with a motocross track between 1977 and 1985.

In 1988 the Bryar family sold the entire park to Bob Bahre who shut down the racing program the following year and completely renovated and rebuilt the facility including the track and road courses, the grandstands, and most of the buildings.

Bryar, as it existed between 1960 and 1985 is entirely gone, replaced with New Hampshire International Speedway, a modern NASCAR-type mile paved oval and a re-drawn road course.

Photo: Bob Manley

Map: 1987

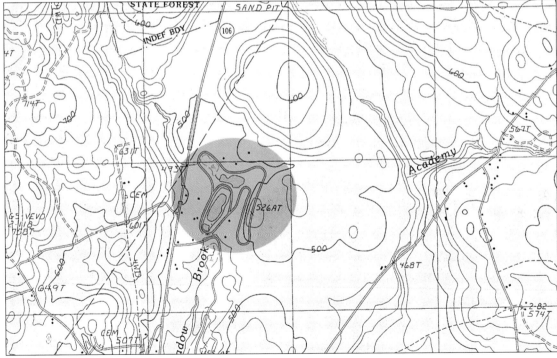

Granite State Park, Dover, New Hampshire

Granite State Park, five miles north of Dover, New Hampshire, was a 1-mile dirt oval track that opened in about 1930 and featured races by mostly independent associations. Doc Morris held the lap record there for the mile distance set in 1936, the year Ray Lowell was killed there. The track was cut to 1/2-mile in 1942 and ran that way until it closed in 1948.

Photo: Joseph Freeman

Map: 1956

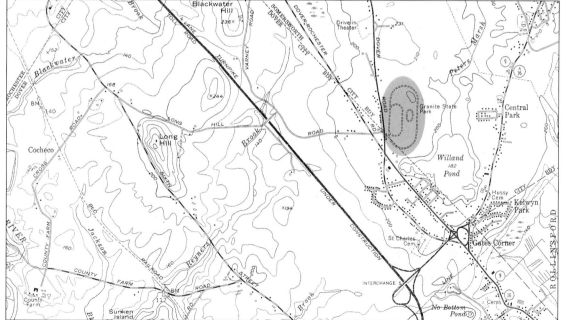

Rockingham Speedway, Salem, New Hampshire

Rockingham Park was a 1-mile horse track built by Bet-A-Million John Gates and August Belmont II in 1906. The track opened on June 28, but the state of New Hampshire quickly shut down open betting and racing ceased three weeks later. Shuttered to wagering, the track became the site of the New Hampshire Fair and held several auto races in 1912 and probably more races in other years. During World War I the U.S. Army used the track as a bivouac site for the 14th Engineer Regiment. Boston auto race promoter and ex-Indianapolis driver Jack LeCain leased the track for auto racing in 1925 and extended it to a mile and a quarter, running a successful race on July 4, won by Ralph DePalma. Thus emboldened, LeCain and his investors then built a 1 1/4-mile board track on the site, with banks soaring to 49 degrees on the turns. Despite a rainout on Columbus Day, the first race on the boards was a financial success as Peter DePaolo, shown here in the No. 12 Duesenberg, won a 250-mile race at 125 mph before a crowd of 70,000.

In 1926 Earl Cooper easily won a 200-mile race in July. During the rest of the year the racing at Rockingham was excellent, but financial troubles loomed. The track was already starting to deteriorate. In October, Harry Hartz was seriously hurt in the last race of the 1927 season and in 1928 the final race of the year had to be halted as the track began to disintegrate. No one took up the race dates AAA assigned Salem for 1929.

In 1930 Lou Smith bought the fairgrounds for a turf syndicate and put the oval back to its original 1-mile length on dirt. Three more auto races were held there in 1931 and 1932, but after that it was reserved for the horses, which still run there very successfully in 2002.

Photo: Joseph Freeman

Map: 1965

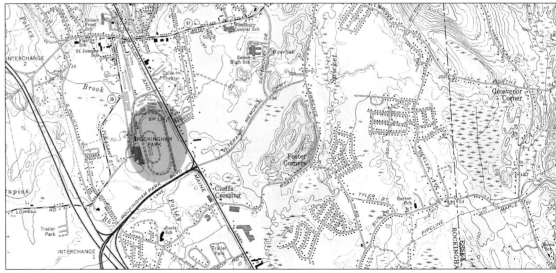

Safford Park, Keene, New Hampshire

The original Cheshire County Fairgrounds were built in South Keene around 1900 but sometime after 1906 they were moved down Route 12 about a mile and a half toward Swanzey, where a typical 1/2-mile dirt track was built that came to be called Safford Park. Big cars of groups such as the New England Auto Racing Association ran there. As seen in this photograph, independents such as Carpenter, Gardner, Trinque, Randall and Chet Conklin raced there from the early thirties, despite three fatalities in the first three races of 1938. The track lay idle from 1948 until 1953 when the Triangle Racing Association brought its stock cars to Keene, then later the Monadnock Stock Car Racing Association took over until the track closed for lack of interest in 1961.

Photo: Joseph Freeman

Program and poster: Author's Collection

Map: 1937

KEENE N.H.

SAFFORD PARK

CHAMPIONSHIP AUTO RACES

NATION'S DEATH-DEFYING DRIVERS
HAIR RAISING
STUNTS - THRILLS

55¢ SUNDAY **OCT. 3**
INCLUDING TAX

Races Start at 2:30 p.m.

RAIN DATE SUN. OCT. 10

FREE PARKING   SANCTION N.E.R.A.

MIDDLETOWN •BOX 328 • MARLBOROUGH, NH 03455

OFFICIAL PROGRAM

NORTH EAST

AUTO RACES

SAFFORD PARK,   KEENE, N. H.

Sunday, October 19

Sanctioned By

North East Racing Association, Inc.

1011 Main Street,   Waltham, Mass.

RACE OFFICIALS

PHIL MAYS, Needham, Mass. .... MANAGER
AL TOCCI, Needham, Mass. .... STEWARD
JACK PENKETH, Waltham, Mass. .... FLAGMAN
WINNIE SPURR, Reading, Mass. .... ANNOUNCER
LINCOLN GRASSO, Needham, Mass. ..... TRACK MGR.
DR. DAVID MANN, Needham, Mass. .... TIMER
LEROY H. WAGNER, Brattleboro, Vt. .... JUDGE
GEORGE GRANT, Greenfield, Mass. .... JUDGE
LONNIE PORTER, Waltham, Mass. .... JUDGE
Metro Sound Systems, Newton Upper Falls, Mass.

•

"PRICE 10 CENTS"

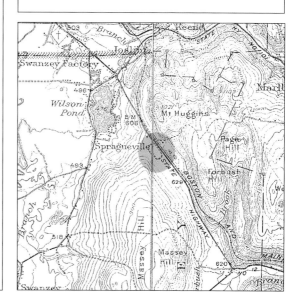

Dover Speedway, New Jersey

Dover Speedway was an oiled 1/2-mile dirt track just off U.S. Route 46 on the east side of town, next to the Dover Tank & Stack Company that owned the land. It was begun in 1932 by Abner Lipman who hired Harry Ahrens of Paterson as his promoter. The opening race, for AAA big cars, was held May 30, 1933. Big car, midget and stock car auto races were run at Dover sporadically until 1954. Sanctioning groups included AAA, the Garden State and the Atlantic associations.

The Esposito brothers, who owned the Tank & Stack Company, took the track over after World War II. It closed in 1954 after the grandstands collapsed twice. In the photograph the car at left is the Peters Offy driven by Mark Light. The dark No. 16 car is the Matera HAL of Frankie Bailey while Ted Horn prepares to get aboard "Baby" in the second row.

Photo: EMMR

Map: 1946

Flemington Speedway, New Jersey

The 25-acre Flemington Fairgrounds were built in 1856 by the Hunterdon County Agricultural Society, which by 1890 could not support its costs and sold the track to horse racing interests. In 1910 the Flemington Fair and Carnival Association bought the 1/2-mile dirt track facility and used it for motorcycle races followed in 1915 by auto racing. Ira Vail won the first race, an AAA-sanctioned affair. The present grandstands were erected in 1917 and the grounds expanded to 51 acres. In 1966 the track itself was expanded to a 5/8-mile square shape which was paved in 1991.

Drivers Chet Gardner and Dick Tobias were killed at Flemington.

In the photograph of midgets at Flemington in 1946, four fans have climbed into a backstretch tree for a better view.

Economics and opposition from the Hunterdon Medical Center across Route 31 halted racing in 2000. Paul Kuhl, the last racing promoter and president of the Fair and Carnival Association, plans to turn the site into either an industrial park or a shopping mall. A citizens group would like to preserve the historic track for bicycling and skating and other events, as Fair Oaks Park.

The track, though closed to racing, hosted vintage meets in 2002 while the debate raged over the eventual disposition of the property.

Photo: EMMR

Map: 1970

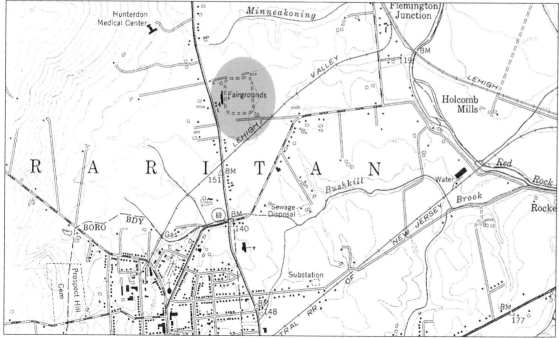

Gasoline Alley, Paterson, New Jersey

At East 29th Street in Paterson, between 17th and 18th Avenues, was a double row of garages, put up early in the century to store the new-fangled autos that many of the silk mill workers were buying to replace their horses. Whether the Gasoline Alley comic strip took its name from the alley in Paterson or it was the other way around, the row of garages soon acquired that title. Racing people moved in, including West Coast star Ted Horn.

Visiting drivers from all over the U.S. stayed there in rented quarters while they raced at Nutley, Woodbridge or HoHoKus. A young Chris Economaki became a "go-fer" for many of the visitors, eager to give directions to the track in exchange for a ride to the races.

Willy Belmont opened the Gasoline Alley Tavern at 838 Market Street and soon it was a popular racers' hangout. Fred Post had his race car upholstery shop there and Pappy Hough built his "Three Little Pigs" in Gasoline Alley. Dick Simonek ran a machine shop there along with J&J Electric, Dick O'Dea's outboard shop, a cycle shop, and garages for a local hot rod club. Ken-Mar Machine took over a space in the 1950s and Frankie DelRoy's Speed Shop was not far away on Route 46.

The Alley survived into the early 1990s, but by the end of the century the area had been cleared for new light industrial construction. It was the end of an era.

Photo: Bruce Craig
Maps: 1949

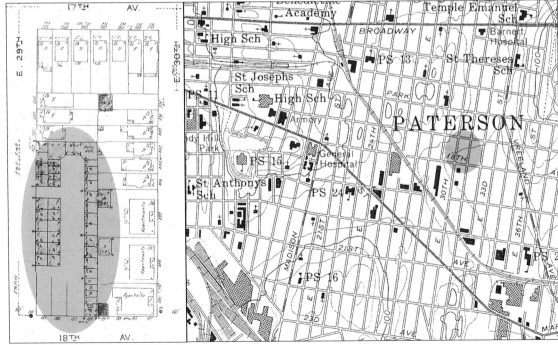

Hinchliffe Stadium, Paterson, New Jersey

Hinchliffe Stadium was built in 1932 on Monument Heights at the Falls of the Passaic River at a cost of $200,550, partly on an old Dutch Reform burial ground and partly on land bought from the Society for Useful Manufacturers that had been founded by Alexander Hamilton. It was dedicated in September 1932 as a football and baseball field for the planned Paterson High School named for Paterson Mayor John V. Hinchliffe.

The 1/5-mile cinder track was a natural for speedway motorcycles, which began racing there in 1934. Interest in motorcycle racing faded, and there was no racing from 1936 through 1938, but when the Nutley, New Jersey track was closed in 1939, its promoter, Jack Kochman, paved Hinchliffe and reopened it for racing under AAA sanction. The stadium was then chiefly a midget track, but stock cars took over in 1950 and ran there for the last two years the track operated. Because of land subsidence the stadium has been derelict for some years and in 2002 a decision was pending in Paterson to renovate it and create a nature preserve downstream at the Falls.

Photo: Bruce Craig

Map: 1968

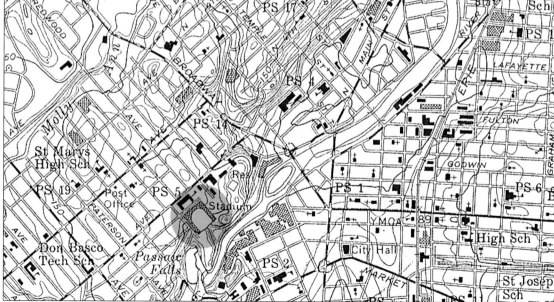

67

HoHoKus Speedway, New Jersey

Promoters built Bergen County Park in 1906 with a 1/2-mile trotting track located on Race Track Road within the loop of the present Arbor Drive, just west of Route 17. It was first used for auto racing in 1912. The track ran in the 1920s under a succession of independent clubs, but in 1934 Jack Kochman secured an AAA sanction that attracted drivers of the caliber of Ted Horn, Bob Sall and Tommy Hinnershitz. Known by then as HoHoKus Speedway, it was quite successful over the succeeding four years.

One of the fans it attracted from the nearby town of Ridgewood was a young Chris Economaki who began his career by selling the Bergen Herald racing supplement at the track. Chris, of course, went on to become editor of the paper, now *National Speed Sport News*. On July 4, 1938, Henry Guerand and Vince Brehm locked wheels and spun through the pits. Starter Francis Fanning was seriously hurt and two spectators, including a ten year old boy, were killed when Guerand's car catapulted off the track into a parked car. The crash ended racing at HoHoKus.

Photo: Joseph Freeman

Map: 1940

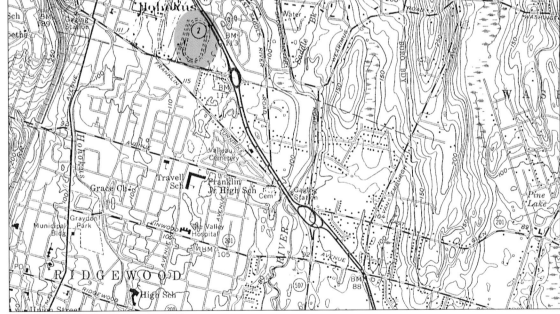

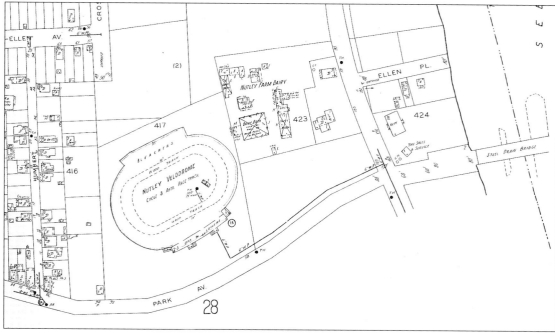

Nutley Velodrome, Nutley, New Jersey

The Nutley Velodrome was a 1/7-mile wooden track, banked to 45 degrees on the turns, built in 1933 for bicycle racing at a cost of $25,000. The site was an abandoned quarry and garbage dump on Park Avenue. Attracting headliners such as France's Alfred Letourner, the Velodrome became the top cycling track in the U.S., but interest in bicycle racing was waning and the Velodrome closed in the middle of the 1937 season.

Jack Kochman looked at the abandoned Velodrome and decided it would make an exciting midget track. The opening race on April 3, 1938, fulfilled that prescription. Over the next two years the hottest hot-shoes in the country raced there including Bill Schindler, Tommy Hinnershitz and Duke Nalon. The crowds were huge and the racing was more than exciting; it was deadly, killing three drivers in 60 race meets.

The last race came on August 26, 1939, when Carl Hattel was killed in the Pat Warren Offy. The town shut down the track and although there was an attempt to revive bicycle racing there in 1940, it was unsuccessful and the track was demolished in February 1942. Nutley built a park and playground on the site in 1950, named after Father Glotzbach, a priest who worked with troubled children.

Photo: Philip Harms
Map: 1939

Trenton Fairgrounds, New Jersey

The Trenton Fairgrounds were built in 1888 and the first auto races on record were held there in 1900. The original 1/2-mile dirt track was lengthened to a mile in 1946, then paved in 1957. The track ran AAA, IMCA, ARDC, USAC, URC and NASCAR races, among others. Trenton was the site of a 250-mile midget race in 1960, the longest ever run at that time—in fact a few special 22-gallon "Trenton Tanks" were built for the Kurtis midgets as a result. In 1969 the track was re-built into a "peanut" shape, extending it to 1 1/2-miles, in order to run USAC championship events, as was the case with this one on September 21, 1969. The fairgrounds were demolished in 1983 for an industrial and industrial arts park. Only a few fragments of the older buildings remain today.

Photo: EMMR

Map: 1970

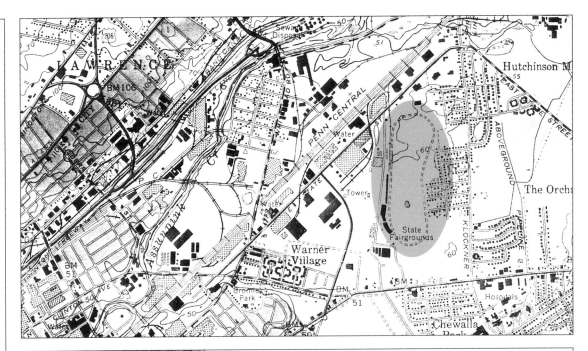

70

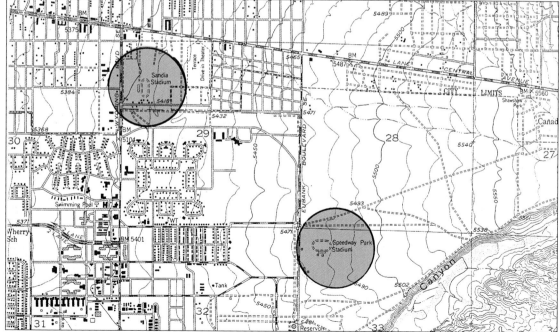

Speedway Park, Albuquerque, New Mexico

Speedway Park was a 3/8-mile dirt track built by the Heisers in 1950 on Eubanks Boulevard east of Albuquerque.

The local Unser family were the stars of the New Mexico Auto Racing Association and had been racing stock cars at the nearby Sandia Stadium. Frank Crosby, a stunt driver with Jimmy Lynch Death Dodgers show, was brought in as the Sandia promoter. When Sandia was torn down in 1955 NMARA moved their races to Speedway Park, and the Heisers asked Frank Crosby to take the track over from the association.

Because of fights between drivers, Speedway Park had only nine cars turn out for the first race of the season. Crosby recalled standing at the pit gate with a paint brush changing the numbers on the cars to give the crowd the idea that there were more cars on hand. Crosby staged a bull fight (the bull survived), ostrich races, camel races, and bear wrestling to keep the interest up.

The Unsers won a lot of the races and were involved in a lot of pit fights at the track. Jerry Unser won the 1955 late model stock car championship there and Al Unser Sr. won it in 1957. Casey Luna won the 1955 and 1956 modified championships and later became Lieutenant Governor of New Mexico.

USAC midgets raced at Speedway park on 1963, with drivers such as Indianapolis winner Parnelli Jones, Jim Davies and Roger McClusky. Al Unser Jr. began his racing career at Speedway Park in the mid-1970s.

Photo: Frank Crosby

Map: 1954

Bridgehampton, New York

Bridgehampton, at nearly the outer end of Long Island, was host to road racing first from July 1915 until 1920, with the races run along Sunrise Highway as part of the annual Firemen's Carnival. The participants, in Ford Model Ts, an Essex and the like, were hardly headline news, yet they established memories that, 30 years later, led to a resumption of racing with somewhat more exotic vehicles.

By 1949 the Hamptons were home to several wealthy sports car owners. Led by Alec Ulmann, they revived road racing that June on a 4-mile highway circuit. Entrants included Cameron Argetsinger, Briggs S. Cunningham and Miles Collier. A crowd of 25,000 watched George Huntoon win in a 1936 Alfa Romeo originally bought to run at Roosevelt Raceway. Cunningham's Ferrari failed to finish. John Fitch, soon to become better known, came in fifth in an MG in the light car event.

Robert Wilder, of Palmer, Massachusetts was killed in a practice run in 1953, and four years later, New York State banned racing on the streets. A new group, including Smith Hempstone Oliver, automotive curator at the Smithsonian Institution, Henry Austin Clark Jr., and George Weaver put together money to build a private, 2.8-mile road course off Millstone Road north of Bridgehampton Village.

Eventually funds to maintain and improve the track ran short. Objections to the noise of race cars from distant neighbors was a constant problem, finally leading to a crippling decibel limit from the town of Southampton. In 1999 real estate speculation finally converted the track to expensive homes with fine views of Long Island's Noyack Bay.

Photo: 1949 race

Maps: 1949 course, 1957 closed course

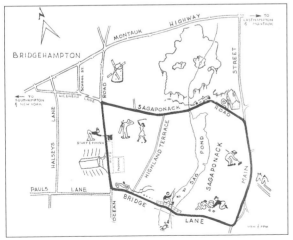

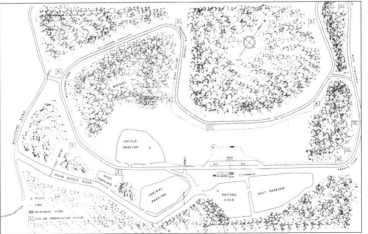

Buffalo Civic Stadium, New York

The 45,748-seat Roesch Stadium was built on Best Street in 1935 as a WPA Depression-era make-work project. It was later re-named Buffalo Civic Stadium. Racing of midgets began on a 1/4-mile cinder track in May 1940. By the end of that summer it was paved with asphalt. The midgets continued to compete at Buffalo for several years after World War II, followed by stock cars that ran until the end of 1959 when the name was changed to War Memorial Stadium.

The Buffalo Bills had played football in the Stadium since 1946, but when they became an NFL team the races were booted out as improvements were made to the field. When the Bills built a new stadium in 1973 the old field, by then known as Rockpile, sat little used and it was finally demolished in 1988 in favor of a recreational field where only a few decorative pillars remain from the old stadium.

Photo: Bob Deull
Map: 1955

Freeport Municipal Stadium, New York

The Freeport Municipal Stadium was built in 1931 as a reflection of the enthusiasm for sports of all kinds that had developed in the 1920s. It had a cinder track of 1/5-mile around a football field and a baseball diamond at its north end.

Bill Tuthill promoted speedway motorcycle racing at the Stadium in 1933 and a year later Milton Ogden scheduled half a dozen races of home-built jalopies. Bill Heiserman promoted the first midget races in 1935 and the little cars would go on to hold 443 meets there over the next 40 years.

Jake Kedenburg, the village Parks Commissioner when the Stadium was built, resigned from that job in 1936 and became the promoter of the races at Freeport for the next 20 years. The cinder track was paved in June 1939. Interrupted by World War II, Freeport resumed racing on Labor Day 1945, as Bill Schindler took the feature in the Caruso Offy before a crowd of more than 12,000 fans. During its history there were only two driver's deaths at Freeport, on succeeding race dates of Tuesday, June 10 (Al Duffy) and Friday, June 13, (Duke Elliott), 1947.

The midgets began to fall out of favor in 1948 and Kedenburg brought stock cars in to share the billing in 1949. In 1974 the track was extended onto the former baseball diamond to provide a 1/4-mile distance. The Stadium closed in 1983 and was torn down in 1989 and replaced by industrial buildings.

Photo: Marty Himes

Map: 1955

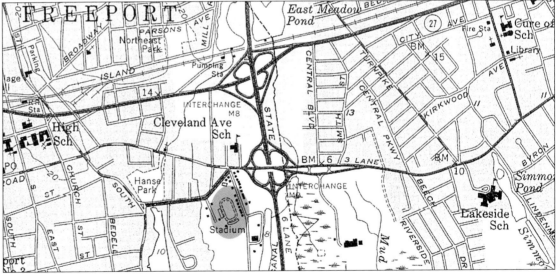

Kingsbridge Armory, Bronx, New York

The 8th Regiment Armory, in the Kingsbridge section of the Bronx, covers an entire city block. Resembling a medieval fortress, it is one of the largest armories in the world. With an interior area of more than 180,000 square feet, it easily encompassed a 1/5-mile racetrack on its concrete floor. In the summer of 1946 Jack Kochman, the innovative promoter who handled racing at HoHoKus, Nutley and Hinchliffe Stadium, secured a winter season lease on the Armory, at Jerome Avenue and Kingsbridge Road. Kochman held a dress rehearsal on November 30 and began midget racing on December 4. The Kingsbridge "Speedrome" was an immediate success, unencumbered in the winter months by competition from outdoor tracks in the metropolitan area.

The first season saw such drivers as Bill Schindler, Ted Tappet, Johnny Ritter, Art Cross and Al Keller win feature races before racing moved outdoors again in April 1947. In 1949 Alexis Thompson and Walter Stebbins took over promotional duties. The racing of midgets and NASCAR stock cars continued at Kingsbridge until 1962.

Although racing there is but a memory, the Armory remains. Completed in 1914 the Romanesque building was placed on the National Register of Historic Places in 1982. It was under reconstruction in 2002 and Bronx county officials were considering whether to convert the building to a community center with a movie theatre, a mall, and a sports facility to train Olympic athletes.

Photo: Bruce Craig

Map: 1956

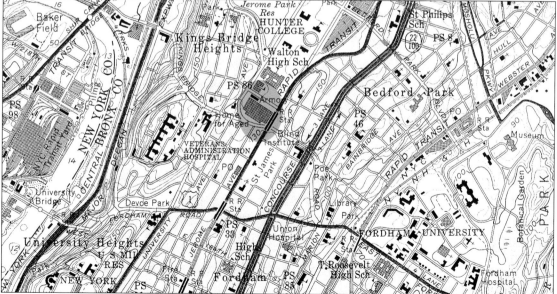

Long Island Motor Parkway, New York

The Long Island Motor Parkway was a 35-mile stretch of 28-foot-wide concrete road built by the Vanderbilt Cup Commission in 1908 to provide a more secure course for the Cup races following the death of a spectator in 1906. In 1904 the course had run over Bethpage Turnpike and in 1906 on Willets Road and North Hempstead Turnpike. The Parkway, as a toll road, was built through farm and marsh land in central Long Island and avoided many of the villages and public roads where crowd control had proven difficult. It was the first road in America to use overpasses at busy intersections.

The Vanderbilt Cup races never used more than the Nassau County portion of the Parkway, which consisted of about 11 miles. In 1908 the 23.45-mile racecourse included Round Swamp Road, Plainview Road, Jericho Turnpike and Old Westbury Road. In 1909 and 1910 the course was trimmed to 12.8 miles, using Broadway and Old Country Road for its westbound leg.

George Robertson was the winner of the October 1908 race in the No. 16 Locomobile, the first American car to win the Cup. Harry Grant won the Cup races in an Alco in 1909 and 1910, after which the Vanderbilt was contested in Savannah, Milwaukee, Santa Monica and San Francisco.

Only fragments of Vanderbilt's racecourse were incorporated into the Nassau County road system, though the Suffolk County portion of the "Motor Parkway" still exists. By 1938—when the author was growing up on Long Island—the western road-bed had been largely abandoned. The Vanderbilt grandstands stood on what is now the 200 block of Orchid Road in Levittown.

Photo: Joseph Freeman

Map: 1908

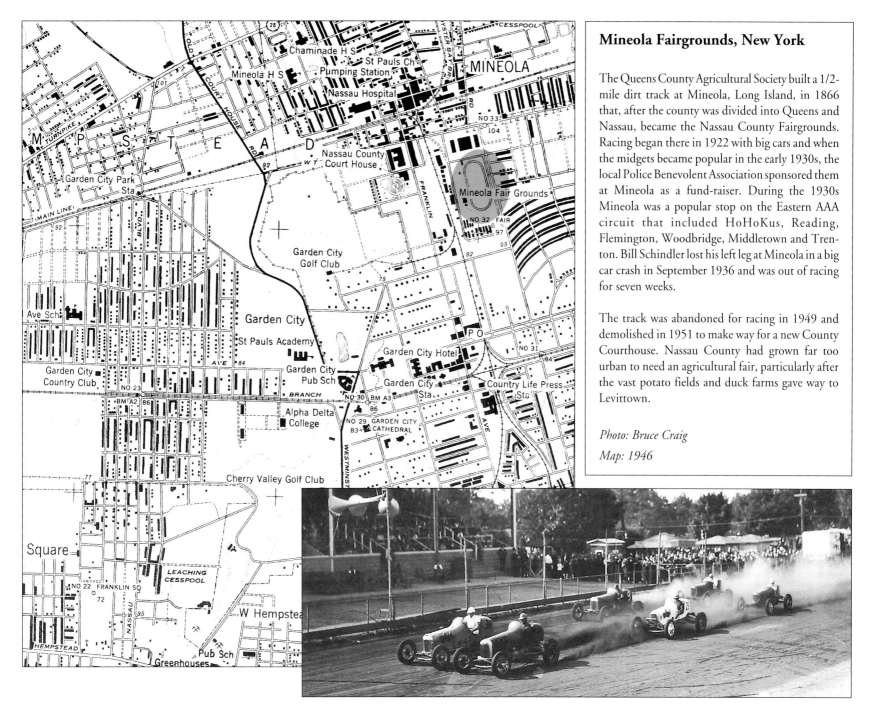

Mineola Fairgrounds, New York

The Queens County Agricultural Society built a 1/2-mile dirt track at Mineola, Long Island, in 1866 that, after the county was divided into Queens and Nassau, became the Nassau County Fairgrounds. Racing began there in 1922 with big cars and when the midgets became popular in the early 1930s, the local Police Benevolent Association sponsored them at Mineola as a fund-raiser. During the 1930s Mineola was a popular stop on the Eastern AAA circuit that included HoHoKus, Reading, Flemington, Woodbridge, Middletown and Trenton. Bill Schindler lost his left leg at Mineola in a big car crash in September 1936 and was out of racing for seven weeks.

The track was abandoned for racing in 1949 and demolished in 1951 to make way for a new County Courthouse. Nassau County had grown far too urban to need an agricultural fair, particularly after the vast potato fields and duck farms gave way to Levittown.

Photo: Bruce Craig
Map: 1946

Polo Grounds, New York

The Polo Grounds were built in 1890 at Coogan's Bluff east of 8ᵗʰ Avenue at 158ᵗʰ Street in Manhattan, across the Harlem River from Yankee Stadium. They were adjacent to a field where polo had once been played, but no horse-mounted riders ever contested on the New York Giants' home field.

In 1940 and 1941 midget auto racing was held there on a 1/4-mile dirt track, and in 1948 Alexis Thompson built a portable wooden track, seen here, that was put up for racing during Giants road trips.

The first board track event attracted a crowd of 25,000, but the races were not nearly as exciting as those at the old Nutley Velodrome had been, and the novelty, and the attendance, wore off. There were problems with the unions that put the track together and took it down for the baseball games, and shortly Thompson sold the track and shipped it to the Rose Bowl in California where it was used slightly more successfully for a year and a half.

The Giants played baseball at the Polo Grounds for 66 years, but moved to San Francisco in 1957. Ed Otto paved a 1/4-mile track around the baseball diamond and held stock car races there in 1958 and 1959. The New York Mets ended racing at the Polo Grounds when they occupied the Polo Grounds in 1962. After the Mets moved to Shea Stadium the stands were finally demolished in 1964 and replaced by public housing.

Photo: Bruce Craig

Map: 1956

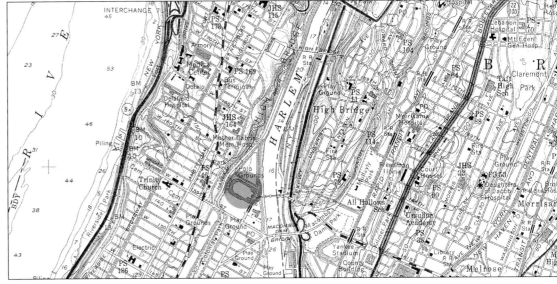

Roosevelt Raceway, New York

It was Roosevelt Field, Westbury, Long Island from which Charles Lindbergh took off from for his epic flight to Paris. In 1936 George Preston Marshall, later owner of the Washington Redskins, built a 4-mile road course of 16 turns at the east end of the field and persuaded George Vanderbilt to offer a new Cup and a $60,000 purse for the winner of an international road race. Top drivers from the U.S., England, Germany, France and Italy were invited.

Tazio Nuvolari won the 1936 race in an Alfa Romeo while Bernd Rosemeyer dominated the 1937 event in a swastika-bedecked Auto Union. Following his victory the tiny Rosemeyer took a seat in the giant permanent trophy. He was killed seven months later trying to set a record on an autobahn near Frankfurt.

Freeport promoters George Morton Levy and Jake Kedenburg tried to lease the Mineola Fairgrounds for harness racing in 1938 but were rebuffed. They turned to the Roosevelt site and laid out a 1/2-mile track there for trotting horses and both big car and midget races. Levy and Kedenburg attempted to offer betting on midget races at Roosevelt in 1938, but local authorities stepped in and stopped them. Tommy Smitten, killed July 27, 1938, was the only fatality in midget racing at Roosevelt. Babe Bower, seen here in the white Bert Krause Offy midget No. 9, won a 300-lap AAA midget championship there in 1939.

The last hurrah for auto racing at Roosevelt came in 1960 when the harness track operators laid out a 1 1/2-mile road course in the parking lots, one stretch of which paralleled the original 1904 William Vanderbilt course and another that actually ran along the line of the runway used by Charles Lindbergh. The peripatetic Chris Economaki was the announcer as Harry Carter in a Stanguellini won the Cornelius Vanderbilt Cup in the SCCA-sanctioned event.

Off-track betting killed Roosevelt Raceway's trotting racing and the track was sold to an investor group in 1984 as a real estate speculation. It closed in 1988 under a cloud of allegations of illegal bond manipulations. The site is now Roosevelt Mall.

Photo: Bruce Craig
Map: 1943

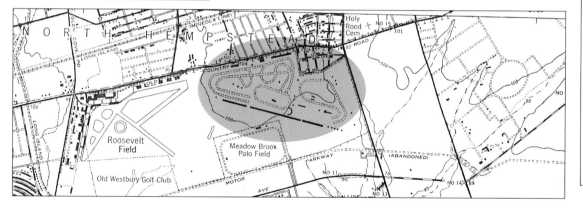

Sheepshead Bay and Brighton Beach, Brooklyn, New York

The Sheepshead Bay and Brighton Beach tracks were within sight of each other on the southwest shore of Long Island. They were built as horse tracks in the boom years after the Civil War. Brighton Beach was built in 1879 by William Engeman and Sheepshead Bay in 1880 by August Belmont II and William R. Travers. Both tracks depended for their income on fees collected from individual bookmakers who, in British style, handled $15 million or so a year in bets. Betting was illegal, but winked at.

Engeman allowed auto racing at Brighton Beach in 1902 as Alexander Winton in his "Bullet" won a ten mile event at an average of 55 mph. Barney Oldfield won the "Championship of the World" there in an October 1904 race against Paul Satori and Maurice Bernin.

New York Governor Charles Evans Hughes had legislation passed putting teeth in the betting laws, which, while it hurt the turf men, made owners more than willing to use their tracks for automobile contests. Brighton Beach saw a series of shorter races for the next two years, with two days of racing over the July 4th holiday in 1911.

When New York State shut down wagering on the ponies in 1910, the Sheepshead Bay track folded. In 1914 Belmont sold the property to a syndicate of wealthy businessmen including Carl Fisher and horseman Harry Harkness, who planned to put a 2-mile brick-paved auto race track on the site. Before construction started the design was changed to build the track of wood.

Harry Grant was killed in a practice accident in October 1915 shortly before the track opened. A total of eight championship races and nine sprint events plus several test runs by auto companies were held there over the next five years.

Though the track made money, its fortunes were intertwined with Harkness' personal difficulties, a messy divorce, gambling and drink. After his death the estate blamed heavy losses conveniently on the track which was sold and demolished in 1920.

Photo: Bruce Craig

Map: 1900

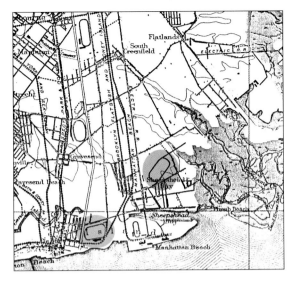

Watkins Glen, New York

The first race of the Sports Car Club of America, formed after World War II, was held in 1948 at the unlikely, bucolic, little village of Watkins Glen, at the foot of Seneca Lake in New York's Finger Lakes region. Cameron Argetsinger, one of SCCA's early members, laid out a 6.5-mile course that ran down Franklin Street, made the turn seen here, climbed Old Corning Hill, then wound through the countryside to a stone bridge across the gorge that gave the town its name, across the New York Central Railroad tracks, then downhill steeply to a sharp turn that came to be known as Milliken's Corner, and back into the village.

The first two races went well with good racing and increasing crowds. Then in 1950 Sam Collier was killed and in 1952 an Allard brushed the crowd standing uncontrolled along Franklin Street and a child was killed. New York State banned racing on public highways and in 1953 the race was moved to a closed road circuit just west of town.

Photos: Alan Isselhard

Map: 1948

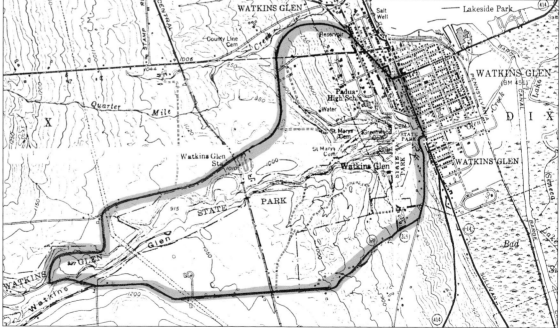

Bismarck, North Dakota

Bismarck was a stop on the barnstorming tours of Barney Oldfield and Will Pickens, but few records remain of those exploits. In 1951, with the midgets still popular on occasional appearances, promoters built a 1/4-mile dirt track east of town off U.S. Route 83. The Central States Race Track, also known as Bismarck Capital Raceway, Capital City Speedway and Fastrax, opened in 1968 east of Bismarck, just south of I-94, and ran stock cars until 1989.

Photo: Carol Holzer

Map: 1976

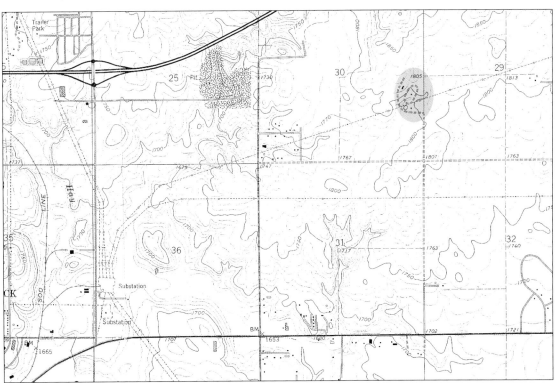

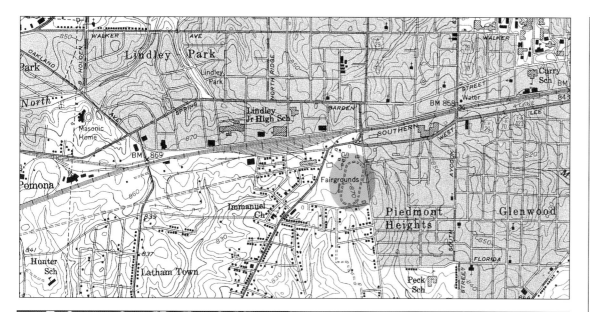

Central Carolina Fairgrounds, Greensboro, North Carolina

The Central Carolina Fairgrounds at Greensboro had a typical fairground 1/2-mile dirt track when it was built in 1920. The earliest racing recorded there came in 1926 and the AAA held big car races there for several years. In 1950 Tommy Hinnershitz won the May race and Duane Carter the October 20-lap feature. In 1953 the track was shortened to 1/3-mile and stock cars raced there until 1957. Another track, a 1/4-mile dirt oval on Route 220, east of town, ran only one season in 1957.

Photo: EMMR

Map: 1951

Charlotte Fairgrounds, North Carolina

While Charlotte is more widely famous for the short-lived board track of 1924 to 1927, there were 34 years of racing at the Southern States Fairgrounds on Sugar Creek Road. The earliest auto races began in 1926 on the 1/2-mile dirt track. In 1936 a traveling troupe of AAA midgets ran ten days of racing on a 1/5-mile oval in the infield. Seen here are Ernie Gesell, No. 6, Cowboy O'Rourke, No. 19 and Vern Fritch's No. 32, all Elto outboard-powered Dreyer-built midgets. The author's father built the access road to the fairgrounds when he was working as North Carolina State Highway Engineer.

When NASCAR was created in 1947, Bill France and Bruton Smith promoted stock car races at Charlotte. Richard Petty won his first Grand National race here in 1960.

The site was cleared in 1960 to make way for a shopping center.

Photo: Bruce Craig

Map: 1948

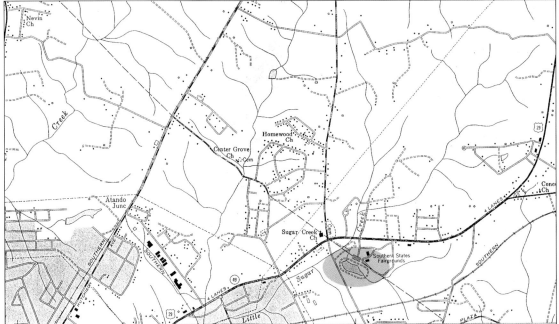

Akron Board Track, Akron, Ohio

In 1926 a group of Akron businessmen headed by Paul Turtin, built a 1/2-mile board track about midway between Akron and Cleveland on Route 8 between the Ascot Park horse track and the present site of the WDAC radio tower. (The horse barns can be seen at the far right in the photo.) Even though the track was banked 45 degrees it was not terribly fast but it was fairly safe. B. Ward Beam was the promoter and Whiz Sloan, a local driver, won the first race on Labor Day 1926, at a speed of 64 mph. The AAA continued to sanction the races, though only one was considered Championship caliber, the June 22, 1930, event, won by Shorty Cantlon in the same Miller-Schofield car in which he finished second at Indy. In 1928, as seen here, Goodyear used the track's infield as the takeoff point of the National Balloon Races. Winners of the Goodyear Nationals qualified for the international Gordon Bennett competition.

Weather, the bane of all the wooden tracks, began to get to the Akron boards by 1930 and the last race was held on September 30 of that year. The track was abandoned and disappeared over the following Depression years.

Photo: University of Akron
Map: 1953

Cincinnati Motor Speedway, Ohio

The usual roster of wealthy investors including R.K. LeBlond, manufacturer of some of the machine tools Harry A. Miller was using to build race cars with in Los Angeles, conjured up a 2-mile banked board speedway for Cincinnati in 1915. The track was built, as were most of the board tracks, of 2x4 boards set on edge. Located at the northern edge of Hamilton County, on a tract bounded by East Kemper, Mosteller, East Crescentville and Reading Roads, contractor Harry Hake finished the track in time for the initial race on Labor Day 1916. Johnny Aitken won the inaugural at a 97-mph average speed.

May of 1917 saw one of the largest festivals in Cincinnati's history, as Indianapolis canceled the "500" because of World War I, which the U.S. entered on April 6. That gave the new Ohio board track the opportunity to host a 250-mile race on Memorial Day, the most prestigious race of the year, which Louis Chevrolet won at speeds of 102 mph, taking home the $10,000 first place prize.

But it was downhill with the termites from there. The last event on the Cincinnati boards was a 48-hour endurance run for the Essex Automobile Company in December 1919, followed by a trip to Federal bankruptcy court. The site became the Sharonville Depot Federal Reservation, which has since been sold for industrial use, including a Penske truck shop and a postal sorting facility.

Photo: Bob McConnell

Map: 1974

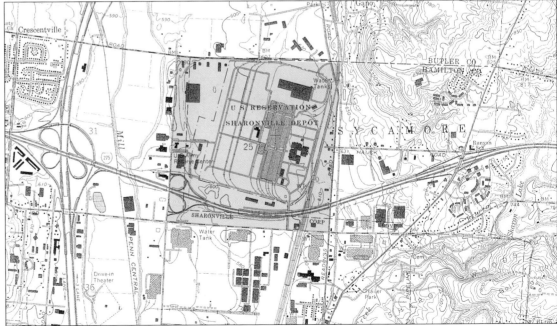

Dayton Speedway, Ohio

Dayton had one of the most active tracks in the U.S. between 1934 and 1982. For much of that time it was the home track for the Central States Racing Association. Built initially as a 5/8-mile flat dirt track, Frank Funk cut it to a 1/2-mile and banked it. Quarter-mile and a 3/8-mile oval tracks were used for the midgets occasionally between 1947 and 1959, but it was best known as a half. CSRA, AAA, AARC and USAC raced there with big cars through 1982. The site is now a landfill.

Photo: Bob McConnell

Map: 1946

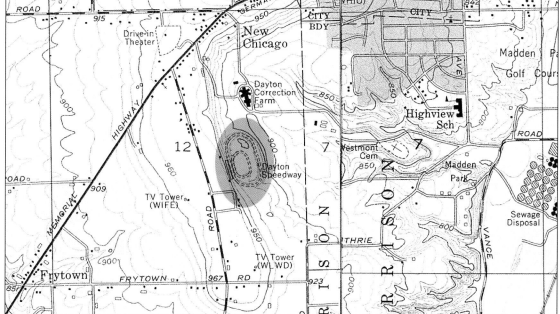

Fort Miami Speedway, Toledo, Ohio

Ft. Miami Speedway was the track at the Lucas County/Fort Miami Fairgrounds, a 1-mile dirt track between Key Street and Michigan Avenue, first used for racing in 1902. Over the years tracks of from 1/4-mile to 3/8-mile were carved into the infield as midgets, big cars and stocks ran there. There was a national AAA midget championship race run at Ft. Miami in June 1940. While attempting to qualify, Bob Swanson, the Gilmore champion, was killed in the Harry Stephens midget.

Racing continued at Ft. Miami through 1957, when the fairgrounds were demolished to make way for the Lucas County Recreation Center.

Photo: Tom Saal

Map: 1951

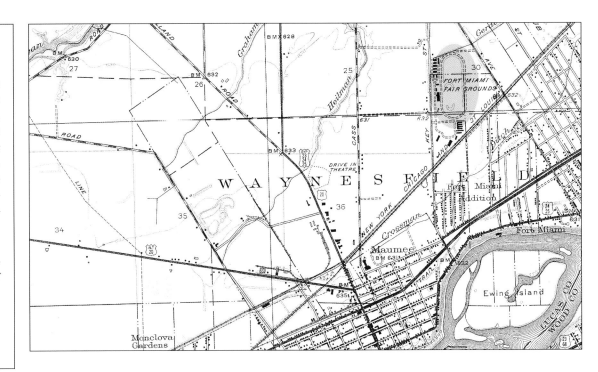

88

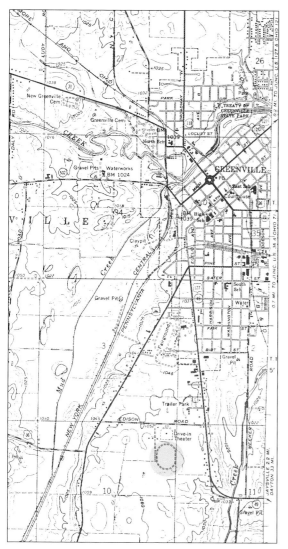

Greenville Motor Speedway, Greenville, Ohio

The Greenville Motor Speedway was a 1/2-mile banked dirt track built in 1921 on Edison Road about a half-mile south of the Darke County Fairgrounds. Ralph Ormsby, publisher of the short-lived racing magazine *Speedway,* (1932-33) based in Cincinnati, reportedly won the first race held there. Greenville was one of the regulars' stops on the CSRA big car and later midget circuit through the 1930s and 1940s. In this photograph Duke Nalon, in the Vance No. 2, leads the field into the first turn.

The two other ovals to the north of the track are horse tracks at the Fairgrounds. The drive-in theatre was built on the property in 1945. Racing continued at Greenville until 1955. Hardly a trace of the track remains save a few seeps of the oil used to settle the persistent dust the racing cars threw up.

Photo: Bob McConnell

Map: 1950

Sportsman Park, Bedford, Ohio

Sportsman Park was built by Al Capone as a dog track. Local legend has it that he located it astride the Summit County - Cuyahoga County line in order to play off local officials against one another in order to allow bookmaking on the races. Although dog races began in 1935, they were shut down the following year. Promoter Joe Byrne then scheduled midget racing on the 1/4-mile dirt track.

After World War II Earl Clay promoted midgets and later stock cars there very successfully. Jimmy Florian was one of the post war stars there. Clay paved the track in 1956, but by the end of that season the track was closed and demolished to make way for Northfield Park, a 1/2-mile harness track that now occupies the site. The Ford Motor Company built its Cleveland Stamping Plant, Walton Hills, on the former airport land adjoining the track to the north.

Photo: John Malone

Map: 1951

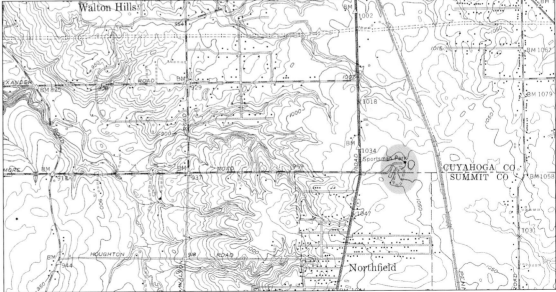

90

The Rubber Bowl, Akron, Ohio

In 1940 the 35,000-seat stadium, called the Rubber Bowl, was completed as a WPA project in the city park adjacent to the 1929 Goodyear Blimp Air Dock at Akron Municipal Airport. "Derby Downs," home of the All-American Soap Box Derby, went up on the southwest side of the Bowl and a 1/5-mile dirt track was built inside it.

Paul Russo won the opening race when midgets came to the Rubber Bowl in 1941. Racing was halted for World War II in early 1942 and resumed in 1945. Midget and stock car racing continued until 1958 while SCCA sports cars raced on the nearby airport from 1954 until 1956. The stadium still exists and is used for University of Akron football games. The Soap Box Derby still holds its International Championships at the Derby Downs incline each July.

Photo: Tom Saal

Map: 1958

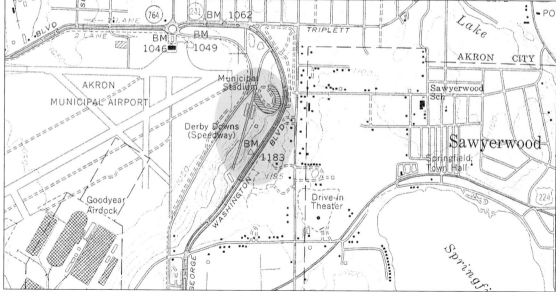

Taft Stadium, Oklahoma City, Oklahoma

Taft Stadium, at Northwest 27th and May Avenue in Oklahoma City, was a high school field that was turned into a prime midget track after World War II. O. D. Lavely, one of the best promoters in the Southwest, and his son, Ray, built a 1/4-mile dirt track around the football field in 1946. Cotton Musick from Wichita won the opener on July 29. Despite the objections of neighbors with sensitive ears, Taft operated sporadically until 1964. Walt Ferrier in 1949 and Bud Hemphill of Pryor, Oklahoma in 1950, were killed at Taft. The Stadium remains today as the Taft Junior High School athletic field.

Photo: Speed Age

Map: 1956

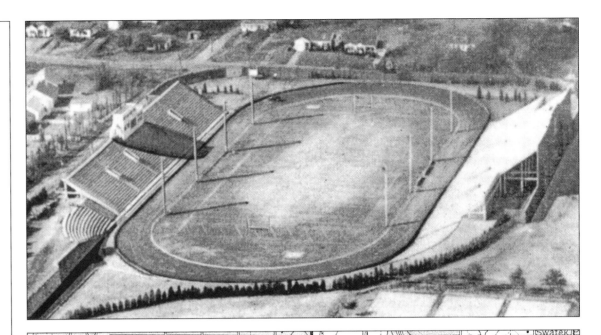

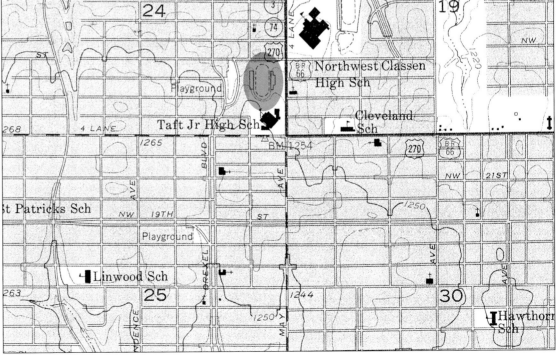

Jackson County Fairgrounds, Medford, Oregon

There was a 1/2-mile fairgrounds dirt track in Medford in 1911, located very close to where Rogue Valley Raceway was built in 1951, at North Central Street and McAndrews. The original track survived until after World War I, when a timber processing plant replaced it.

Seen here are Tip Blume and George Lott in the Newman Racing Team's Stutz' known as the "Yakima Mankillers."

Photo: Joseph Freeman

Map: 1983

Allentown Fairgrounds, Pennsylvania

The Allentown Fairgrounds, at 17th and Liberty Streets, were built in 1889. The track was added in 1901 and the brick and concrete grandstands in 1908. They were host to auto racing at least as early as 1919 when Ira Vail won a feature race there on the 1/2-mile track. It became one of the premier stops on the AAA big car circuit and after 1955, URC races. Bill Schindler was killed at Allentown on September 20, 1952, and Johnny Thomson was killed there on September 24, 1960, in the same car. There was, briefly, an 1/8-mile drag strip at Allentown in 1964. The last oval-track race was held there during Bicentennial celebrations in 1976. The grandstands were reconfigured and a stage was built on the track in 1985 for rock concerts and other entertainment.

The track was not far from Pop Leibensberger's shop on Gordon Street where the famous Gordon Racing Team outboard midgets were built. The track was still intact, though unused, as late as 1987. Mini-sprints ran at Allentown in 1989 on a 1/8-mile oval.

Photo: Bruce Craig

Map: 1964

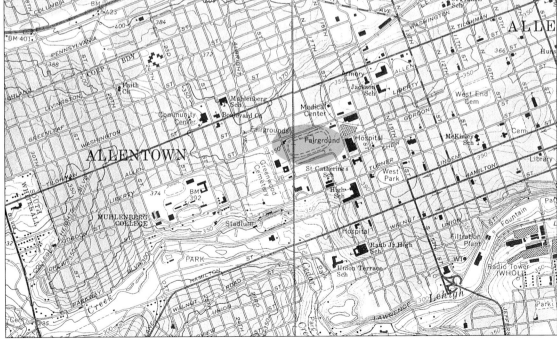

Line up of CARS

Altoona Speedway, Pennsylvania

The Altoona board track, actually located at Tipton, about 12 miles to the north, was a 1 1/4-mile wood oval built on E. B. Dysart's farm between the Little Juniata River and the Pennsylvania Railroad tracks. After it opened in 1923 the track held 100-mile races each Flag Day and Labor Day. Eddie Hearne won the opening race in a 122-cubic-inch Miller. The original boards began to deteriorate by 1927 and the AAA required resurfacing, which was done with chestnut, extending the track's life longer than that of any of the other wooden speedways. The tracks' 17th and last race was held in September 1931. The controlling corporation went under in the wave of bank failures in the Depression rather than due to its own lack of success. Left idle for three years, the western end of the track was undermined by a 1936 flood, then vandalized by squatters living in the track's buildings.

Converted to a 1 1/8-mile oiled dirt track in 1935, Altoona ran seven races over the following five years. After World War II a 1/4-mile track was added in the infield and stock cars and motorcycles raced there in 1952. Part of the property was sold for an industrial site in 1959, and a drag strip was built on the remaining land. By the late 1980s industrial development had all but submerged the last of the property.

Photo: Smithsonian

Map: 1953

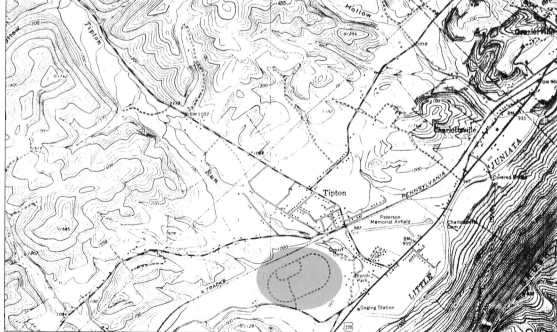

Bloomsburg Fairgrounds, Bloomsburg, Pennsylvania

The Bloomsburg Fair began in 1855 and the 1/2-mile track, like many others, was built for the then-popular trotting races. The first auto races of note were promoted there in 1923 under Horace P. Murphy at the annual Columbia County Fair. Bobby Boone was killed at Bloomsburg in a midget in 1958. Racing was highly popular for 58 years until the premiums for liability insurance became prohibitive in 1985. Randy Mausteller of the SMRC club was the last promoter. There was one more attempt to revive racing on July 11, 1987, but it did not draw enough of a crowd to pay the insurance premiums.

Photo: EMMR

Map: 1947

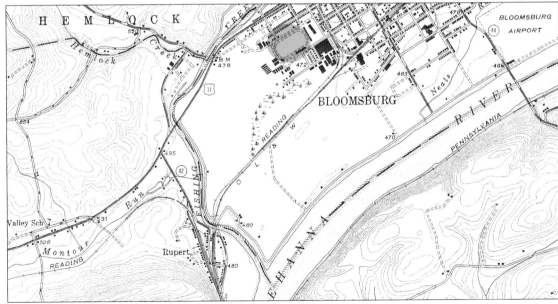

Hatfield Speedway, Hatfield, Pennsylvania

Hatfield Speedway was a 1/2-mile dirt horse track built at the Montgomery County Fairgrounds. The first known auto race was held there in 1922. After World War II midgets ran at Hatfield on a 1/4-mile dirt track in 1952 and 1953. It was back to the 1/2-mile track, then paved, from 1954 through 1959, then a 1/3-mile banked dirt track for the rest of the track's life, which ended in 1967 when it was replaced by housing. A 1/8-mile drag strip operated briefly on the property in the 1960s.

Red Riegel was the master of Hatfield, winning five of five features there in 1961 and a total of 16 races during his career.

Photo: Bruce Craig

Map: 1957

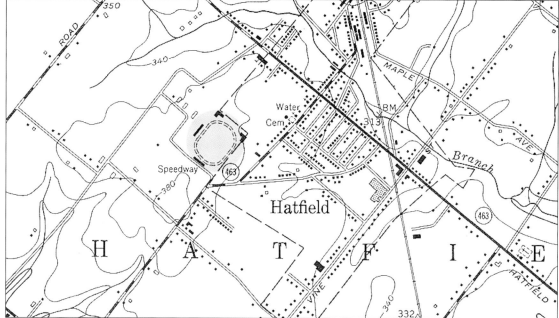

Hershey Park, Hershey, Pennsylvania

Milton Hershey began building Hershey Park in 1907, seven years after he invented the Hershey Bar, adding features and attractions over the years. During the Depression, as part of his own WPA project for Central Pennsylvania, he built the stadium, completing it in 1939. The first midget races were held there on a flat 1/5-mile asphalt track on May 18, 1939. Doc Shanebrook won the first feature race, seen here just after the start.

There was little racing just after World War II, but the ARDC midgets returned to Hershey in 1967 for three years. Bert Brooks, who won the July feature there, was killed at Hershey on Labor Day 1968. The midgets were back again in 1982 and 1983, and TQs ran there in the mid-1980s. But the demand for facilities for rock concerts and other non-racing events led to changes to the track that made auto racing no longer possible. Hershey still hosts the vast Antique Automobile Club of America National Fall Meet during which vintage racing cars make condition runs in the stadium, but it seems unlikely that competitive racing will return there.

Photo: Bruce Craig

Map: 1972

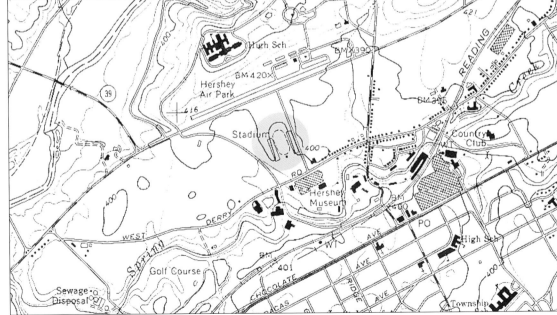

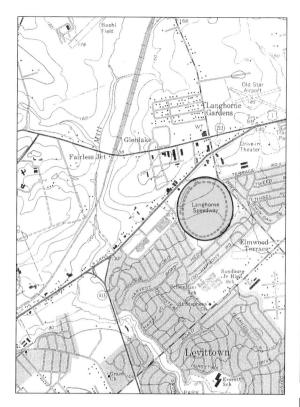

Langhorne Speedway, Pennsylvania

Langhorne Speedway was one of the few 1-mile dirt tracks built solely for auto racing. Used at first in 1926 for sprint races, over its 45 years it hosted champ cars, midgets, motorcycles and stock cars as well. It was known as "The Big Left Turn," since it had no straight-aways, being a near-circle that gave drivers no place to relax for even a moment.

NMRA, an independent group, built Langhorne and ran it for three years (not very successfully). In 1929 Leo Cornell obtained an AAA sanction for Memorial Day. Ralph Hankinson promoted AAA races in 1930 and 1931, followed by Dick Dunn with Hankinson returning in 1934. Hankinson made money with the track, eventually holding big car events each week. Red Crise and Jack Kochman promoted a 100-mile midget championship there in October 1940. Lucky Teter took over the promotion in 1941 and shifted the sanction to CSRA.

After World War II John Babcock bought the track and Jimmy Frattone handled the promotion, running it with CSRA in 1946. After Yellow Jackets closed in Philadelphia, Frattone carved out a 1/4-mile midget track at Langhorne that was used for only three months in 1951. Irv Fried returned the track to AAA sanction and later to USAC racing.

At least 16 drivers and spectators died at Langhorne in its 45 years, including Jimmy Bryan and Mike Nazaruk.

The 1-mile track was paved—many said spoiled—in 1965 when the rear engine revolution came along, but the real estate had become too valuable and the track was sold in 1971 to build a shopping center.

Photo: Gene Ericksom

Map: 1952

Reading Fairgrounds, Pennsylvania

The 1/2-mile dirt track at the Reading Fairgrounds in the suburb of Hyde Park, saw its first recorded auto race in September 1924, a Ralph Hankinson-promoted event won by Grady Garner. Reading was the home track of Pennsylvania big car Champion Tommy Hinnershitz and many famous drivers started and raced there. Lee Wallard, the 1951 Indianapolis winner, suffered career-ending burns at Reading on June 3, 1951, and Jud Larson and Red Reigel were killed there June 11, 1966.

Reading saw its last race on June 29, 1979, before the track was demolished for the Fairgrounds Square Mall.

Photo: Frank Smith

Map: 1956

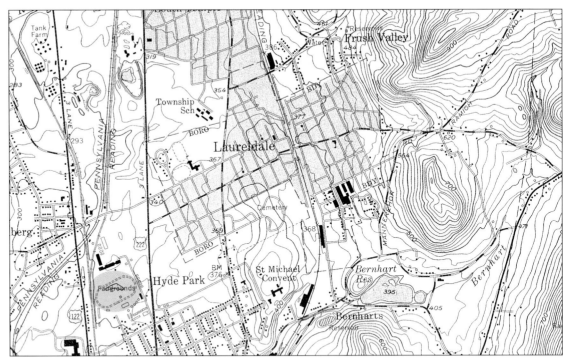

Yellow Jackets Speedway, Philadelphia, Pennsylvania

Bill Heiserman inaugurated midget racing at Yellow Jackets Stadium on Frankford Avenue, home of the local semi-pro football team, in 1935. When the team moved to Erie Avenue and G Street in 1939, Walter Secrist took over the promotion. Both were 1/5-mile dirt tracks. Tommy Hinnershitz, Ronney Householder, Bill Schindler, Buster Warke and other AAA midget stalwarts were headliners there prior to World War II.

Racing at Yellow Jackets continued until the end of the 1950 season when the stadium was replaced by industrial development.

Photo: Bruce Craig
Map: 1949

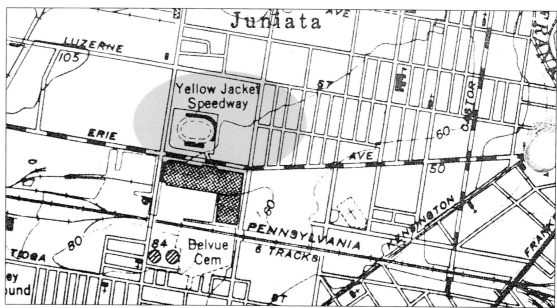

Lonsdale Sports Arena, Rhode Island

Lonsdale was a 1/3-mile, high-banked, paved track, built in 1947 on the shore of the Blackstone River near Route 122 during the height of the midget boom. It was first sanctioned by the Bay State Midget Racing Association, and Bill Schindler won the first feature event on August 13, 1947, in the Caruso Offy No. 2. That October promoter Bill Tuthill brought stock cars to Lonsdale, making it the first time the coupes had run in the north. Fonty Flock won the first stock car race, followed by Buddy Shuman and Red Byron, attracting a crowd that encouraged the formation of NASCAR. AAA sanctioned the track in 1948, but UCOA and then BSRA soon replaced them.

A fall 1955 hurricane caused the Blackstone River to flood, undermining half of the stands. Poor crowds made it financially impossible for the McNultys to rebuild properly and the last race, a midget affair won by Cliff Riggott in the Wozniak Kurtis Offy No. 53, was held on September 30, 1956. The site has since been converted to a shopping center.

Photo: Tommy Caruso

Map: 1949

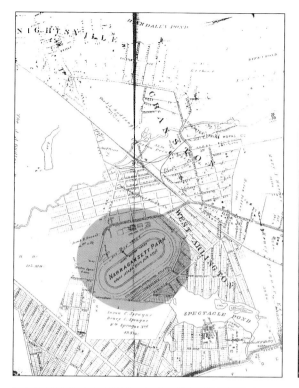

Narragansett Park, Rhode Island

The first auto races ever held on a closed course were run at the Rhode Island State Fair on the old 1-mile dirt horse track at Narragansett Park in Cranston, September 7 through 10, 1896. There was one five-mile heat run each day. A. H. Whiting won the first race in a Riker Electric and also won the overall three-day contest, two heats to one. H. G. Morris in an Electric Wagon & Carriage Co. car won the other heat. The gasoline-powered Duryea, the victor at Chicago ten months earlier, led only one lap of a five-mile heat on the second day of the fair.

These photographs show the Electrics and the gasoline-powered "motocycles," on September 7, lined similar to a horse race for the first of their five-lap sprints.

Narragansett Park had been built for the state fair trotting races in 1867. Its dirt surface was later oiled and it was used for subsequent auto racing until 1919, and torn down in 1925. Fiat Avenue, across Gansett Avenue from Bain Junior High School, still follows the outline of the track.

Photos: Smithsonian
Map: 1900

Columbia Speedway/Fairgrounds Speedway, Cayce/Greenwood, South Carolina

Auto racing became most popular in South Carolina after World War II with the coming of NASCAR, but there was big car racing earlier in the twentieth century. Two of the older tracks that once saw racing in the state were the Columbia Speedway at the fairgrounds in the Cayce section of Columbia and the Fairgrounds Speedway on Laurens Road in Greenwood.

The first recorded race at Cayce, a 1/2-mile dirt track, was in 1932 and there was racing at the annual fair until the outbreak of World War II. Racing resumed after the war and continued until 1970. In 1953 a 1/4-mile dirt track was run there as Palmetto Speedway. It was then paved and used as the New Columbia Speedway until 1977.

In Greenwood the fairgrounds horse track was built in 1935. After World War II big cars ran there for two years, then a 1/4-mile track was built around an adjacent football field that ran until 1968.

Photo: Tom Saal
Maps: Columbia 1972 (left)
Greenwood: 1949 (right)

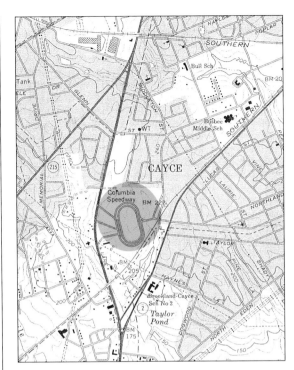

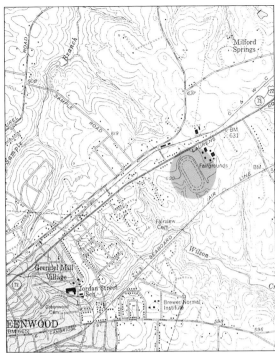

Sioux Empire Fairgrounds Race Track, Sioux Falls, South Dakota

The West Soo Speedway, a 1/2-mile track, was first used for big car racing in 1936. It was located at the fairgrounds in Sioux Falls, built early in the twentieth century. In 1941 the owner, W. H. Lyon, died, and his widow, Winona, deeded the land to the city. The track became known as the Sioux Empire Fairgrounds Race Track. IMCA ran there in 1941, with Emory Collins the big winner.

IMCA sanctioned most of the postwar races with the exception of an AAA sprint car race in August 1953 that was won by Bob Scott and announced by Chris Economaki.

Modified stock cars ran at Sioux Falls until 1987 and a "run whatcha brung" "cheaters" sprint car race was run annually until 1999. In 2000 a permanent stage was erected on the main straightaway in front of the grandstands and the rest of the track was converted into a parking lot.

Photo: Tom Savage
Map: 1971

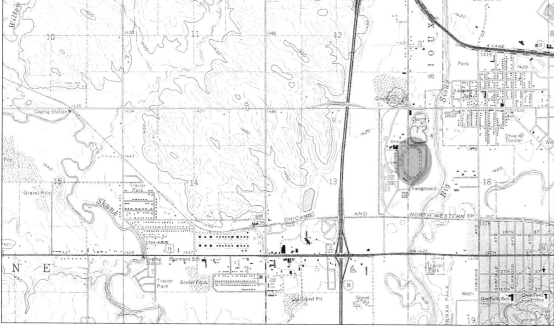

Arlington Downs, Texas

Arlington Downs opened in 1929 as a 5/8-mile dirt horse track, built east of Arlington by W. T. Waggoner, who expanded it to 1 1/16 miles in 1934. Waggoner died in 1936 and Gov. James V. Allred got the Texas legislature to ban betting a year later. The last professional horse race was held at Arlington Downs in 1937.

To fill the void, Waggoner's estate used the track for sprint and jalopy races, air shows, motorcycle races, square dances and Texas hoe-downs. During World War II it was used as an Army motor depot.

The track was soft and developed severe ruts during the races, but Ted Horn won a 100-mile (95-lap) AAA race there in November, 1947. Johnnie Parsons won the last champ race at Arlington on April 24th, 1949. There were shorter AAA events for Indianapolis cars in July 1949 and April, 1950.

The track's greatest day in the sun was at the April, 1950 AAA event when Warner Brothers filmed dirt track scenes there for their racing movie "To Please a Lady," starring Clark Gable and Barbara Stanwyck. Even to this day, Arlington old-timers recall Gable's presence at a party for the Hollywood stars and the race drivers. There was an All-State Association 250-mile stock car race in October, 1950 and the final recorded races at Arlington were a pair of 200-mile IMCA stock car events in 1951.

Waggoner's estate sold the track to a real estate syndicate in 1956 and it was demolished. The contours of the course and some of the trees that surrounded the track may still be seen. A furniture store and a western wear outlet occupy a corner of the tract while the Six Flags over Texas Mall is across route 360.

Photo: Don Radbruch
Map: 1959

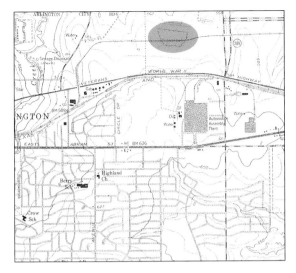

Playland Park, Houston, Texas

Playland Park, a 1/4-mile dirt track built by Sam Fox, opened in 1948 at an amusement park of the same name. It did not become successful until two former Californians, O. D. Lavely and his son, Ray, took over the promotion in 1949. They added a 1/3-mile road course in 1950.

A. J. Foyt began his career at Playland Park in 1953 at the age of 18 and, according to his biography, set fast time the first night out.

Lavely paved the 1/4-mile track in 1957. The last promoter there was Ed Hamblen. The track itself was demolished in 1960. The Playland Amusement Park survived for a few more years, even after construction of the nearby Astrodome. The site, between the present Murworth and Westridge Streets, was cleared in the 1980s. The composite map here shows both Playland, and the Astrodome, built in 1965, which also had auto races for a time.

Photo: Speed Age

Map: 1960

107

Bonneville Salt Flats Circle, Utah

The Bonneville Salt Flats have been used for timed straight-away speed runs since 1914 when Teddy Tetzlaff drove the Blitzen Benz 141 miles per hour there. In the upper photograph John Cobb readies his Railton Mobil Special for straightaway runs in 1946. Less familiar have been the endurance runs made on the salt, along the circumference of a ten-mile circle marked by flags, a line of road oil and, at night, burning flares.

Ab Jenkins laid out the first endurance run circle in 1932 and then put 2,710 miles on a Pierce Arrow there in 24 hours. In 1934, he ran a new, modified Pierce Arrow, seen in the lower picture, for 24 hours at an average of 127.229 miles per hour, and made his final endurance run in 1956 in a Pontiac, covering 2,841 miles in the 24 hours.

While the straightaway runs continue to this day at Bonneville and, though other, smaller oval courses have been used, the circle has disappeared, washed away by the winter rains and never re-established after 1956.

Photo: Mark Dees Collection,

Marvin Jenkins Collection

Map: 1939

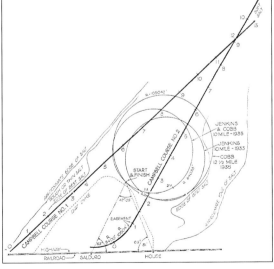

Utah Fairgrounds, Salt Lake City, Utah

In 1904 the Deseret Agricultural & Manufacturing Society built a 1/2-mile track on their fairgrounds at North Temple and 9th West (that included a grandstand, box office and judges stand), in time for Barney Oldfield, seen here leaving a trail of dust in his old home town, to set "a new world's record" in the Ford No. 999. The next recorded races came in 1907, followed by Oldfield shows in 1910 and 1914 with the front-drive Christie. There was an AAA 100-miler there in 1924. Big car racing continued sporadically at the Fairgrounds in the 1930s and a 1/4-mile dirt track known as "Intermountain Speedway" was added in 1940. The track was paved after World War II and lasted until 1972.

The rodeo arena now occupies the site's 1/4-mile track and no trace remains of the larger oval.

Photo: Utah State Historical Society

Map: 1969

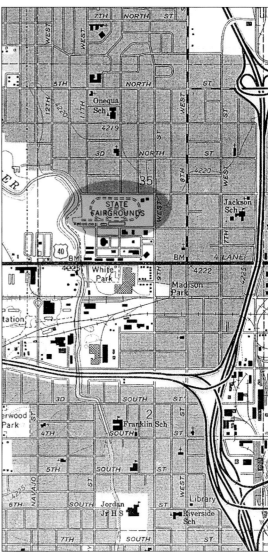

Champlain Valley Exposition, Essex Junction, Vermont

The Champlain Valley Exposition, founded in 1923, ran big cars on a 1/2-mile dirt track during the annual fall fair beginning in 1930 under AAA sanctions promoted by Ira Vail. (Not only the cars were racy. Sally Rand and Gipsy Rose Lee also performed at the fair.) Aside from the interruption generated by World War II, fair date racing continued until 1977 when Sam Nunis put on the last races with ARDC midgets and URC sprint cars. In the 1980s the Essex Junction track was host to at least a few vintage race shows where drivers could experience the thrill of "steering with the throttle" on an old-fashioned dirt surface, not modern hard clay.

Photo: Champlain Valley Exposition

Map: 1948

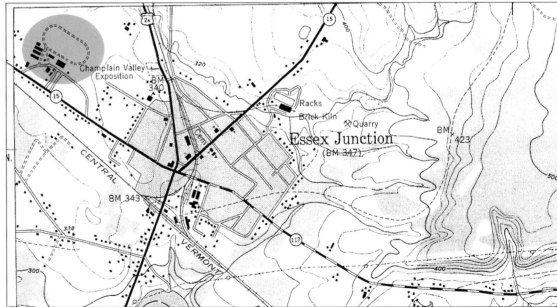

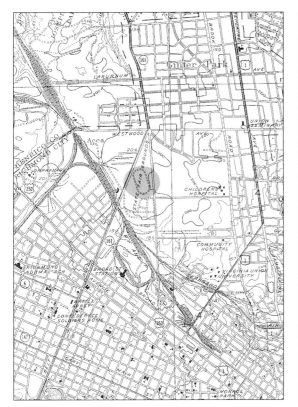

Richmond State Fairgrounds, Virginia

The old Virginia State Fairgrounds of the Atlantic Rural Exposition were used for auto racing at least as early as 1907. They stood between what is now North Boulevard and Hermitage Road at Sherwood Avenue, the present site of Parker Field, a minor league ballpark, easily visible from I-95.

The original 1-mile track was replaced by a 1/2-mile oval in 1919. Jimmy Kline, one-time builder of the Kline Kar passenger vehicle, was the promoter of the Labor Day races there from 1921 until 1941. Most of the headliners of the AAA raced at Richmond including, in the late 1930s, Ted Horn. Bill France drove big cars there as well, for a "guarantee" of as little as $15.

In 1947 the track was shifted to the new Fairgrounds at Strawberry Hill, the present site of Richmond International Raceway. The old track was demolished and replaced by Parker Field in 1954.

Photo: EMMR

Poster: Author's Collection

Map: 1939

111

Virginia Beach Speedway, Virginia

Virginia Beach Speedway, at the intersection of Witchduck Road and Virginia Beach Boulevard, was a 3/8-mile track scraped out of the Virginia sand in 1948 by Paul Sawyer (later to become the owner of the Richmond International Raceway) and driver Joe Weatherly. The track was later known both as Joe Weatherly Speedway and Chinese Corners Speedway and ran mostly stock cars, though SCODA sports cars ran there (for money) in 1955. Jim Creech was the last promoter before the track closed in 1960. Today Virginia Beach School administration buildings stand on the site along with an auto parts store and a Rally's hamburger stand.

Photos: Len Ashburn

Map: 1955

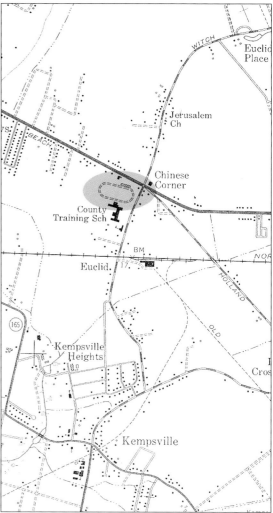

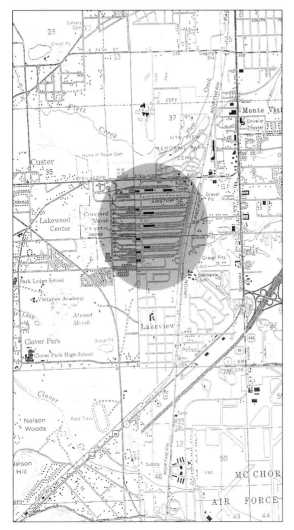

Tacoma Speedway, Tacoma, Washington

Tacoma Speedway, a 2-mile dirt track, was built in 1914 and raced for a year before local sponsors raised the money to build the Pacific Coast Speedway, a wooden track of the same length. Located on Steilacoom Boulevard, the track was accessible to downtown Tacoma, seven miles away, by road, railroad, and even by steamers from across Puget Sound.

The board track was originally planned to have asphalt pavement over the wood, and narrow gaps were left between the planks to anchor the tar. On July 4, 1915, Barney Oldfield paced the first race in a Buick. The track was quickly marked by tragedy when "Coal Oil Billy" Carlson, a Maxwell driver and his mechanic, Paul Franzer, died as their car sailed off the 18-foot-high banks. Grover Ruckstell later won in a Mercer.

Tacoma was quite successful as board tracks went, lasting eight seasons before the timber deteriorated beyond usefulness.

After the boards rotted away the site was used for a Navy landing strip, then the Crawford Marsh U.S. Naval Depot and, after World War II, it was converted to the Clover Park Technical College.

Photo: Joseph Freeman

Map: 1948

Bennings Race Track, Washington, D.C.

The Washington Jockey Club built a 1/2-mile horse track on a meadow at Deanwood, near the village of Bennings, on the eastern shore of the Anacostia River, in 1885. E. A. Brooks, the manager of the Jockey Club, allowed auto racing at least as early as September 5, 1905. There was racing there sporadically for the following 35 years, with the first AAA Contest Board sanction granted in 1911. In 1916 and 1917 Brailey Gish defeated all comers in the Weightman Special. The last races on record were held in 1937, shortly before the Jockey Club abandoned the track.

The track was between the present Hayes and Jay Streets, northeast, now the current location of the Mayfair Mansions public housing. In fact, the present streets follow the curve of the old racetrack and the smokestacks of the Washington Pepco power plant still loom behind the site.

Photos: Library of Congress

Map: 1906

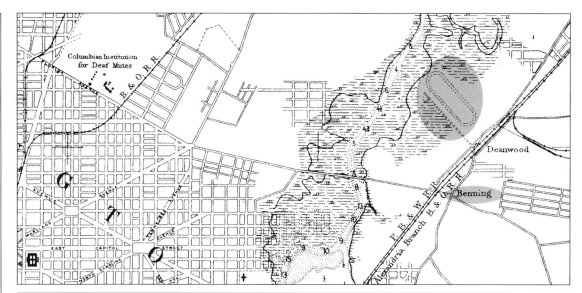

114

Wheeling West Virginia Fairgrounds, Wheeling, West Virginia

The first recorded automotive competition at the Wheeling West Virginia Fairgrounds track was an AAA race in 1911, though there may have been races there earlier. Records are fragmentary but there were AAA races in Wheeling and elsewhere in the area, sponsored by the Ohio Valley Auto Club in the fair season in 1915 and throughout the 1920s. AAA stars such as Ted Horn appeared from 1938 through 1940, and in 1941 under CSRA banner.

The oval on Wheeling Island is now purely a pari-mutuel horse track and the alignment has been revised since this 1956 map was surveyed.

Photo: Bob McConnell

Map: 1956

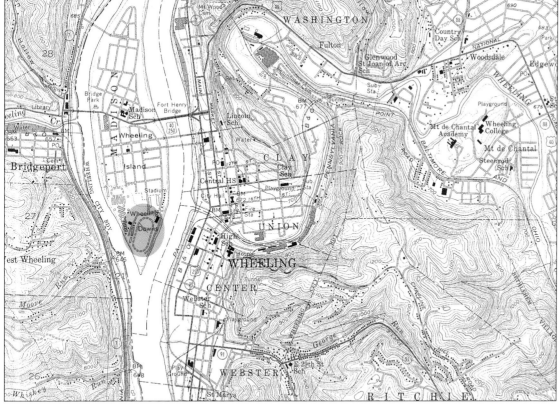

Ozarkee County Fairgrounds, Cedarburg, Wisconsin

The Ozaukee County Fairgrounds were built in the fork between Sheybogan Road and Washington Avenue, early in the twentieth century and auto racing came to Cedarburg in 1914. Also known as Cedarburg Speedway, the 1/2-mile track was cut to 1/3-mile in 1941 and the fairgrounds re-named Firemen's Park.

Seen here in an early race lineup are a pair of entries from the Marchese brothers who later owned midgets and Indianapolis cars and promoted AAA races at the nearby Milwaukee mile track. Racing continued with late models and modifieds until 1979 when the firemen found they could make more money with flea markets than racing. John Kashian was the last promoter there.

Photo: Steve Zautke

Map: 1959

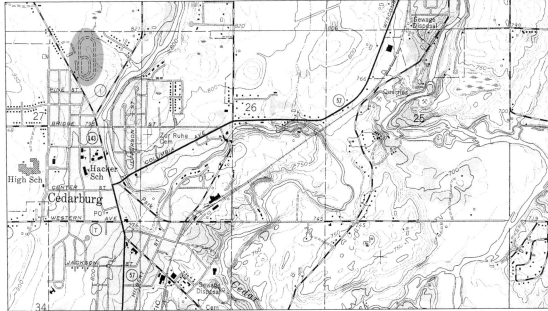

Frontier Park, Cheyenne, Wyoming

The original Cheyenne fairgrounds were moved to Frontier Park in 1908. The first recorded race was held on August 17, 1909, when the Cheyenne Motor Club received an AAA sanction for 50 laps on a 4-mile circuit beginning at the fairgrounds and running out over the prairie. Charles Basle was the winner in an Oldsmobile, followed by a Renault and a Marmon and a Moon. (Ben Loy, trying out that track before the race, was killed and his mechanic injured when their car hit a cow.) The present track was built in 1910 and the first racing at fair time began in 1918.

Cheyenne's racing history is fragmentary, but fair dates appear to have continued into the 1940s. The Frontier Park Fairgrounds still exist off Carey Avenue. Frontier Days, the famous Cheyenne rodeo, is held there yearly.

Photo: Tom Saal

Map: 1961

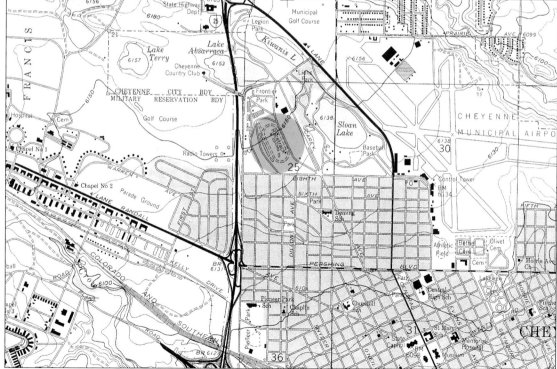

Huracan Stadium, Buenos Aires, Argentina

In November, 1938 a group of American midget drivers including Pappy Hough and Buster Warke were invited to race during the winter in Argentina. The promoters bought several mediocre midgets and transported the entourage to Buenos Aires on the *SS Argentina*. They raced at Estadio Huracan', a soccer stadium in downtown Buenos Aires. Seventeen years later another promoter hired U.S. midget drivers from the West Coast to race at Huracan' during the winter of 1955.

The Club Atelico Huracan is the premier and much-loved soccer team in Buenos Aires, comparable in the U.S. to the New York Yankees or the Dallas Cowboys. Huracan' Stadium still exists, but they do not race automobiles there any more.

Photo: Jack Fox

Maps: 1935

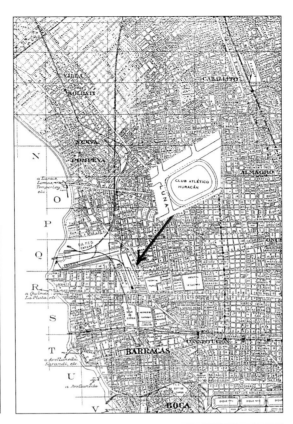

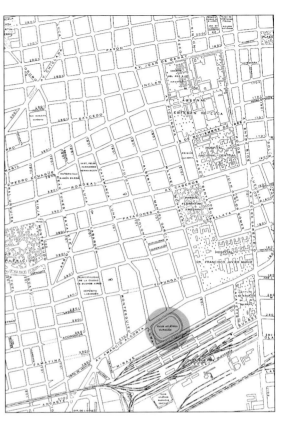

Sydney Showground Speedway, Australia

The Sydney Showground Speedway, a 1-mile cinder track originally known as the Royale, was built in 1926 for speedway motorcycle racing. To this day speedway motorcycles in Australia are not equipped with brakes. The standing start record is 59 seconds.

It was a deadly track, with 28 deaths over 55 years. Midgets (known Down Under as "speed cars"), hot rods and stock cars also ran at Sydney before it closed in 1981. The track was re-opened for eight years in 1988, but was finally closed in 1996, replaced in 1999 for racing, if not in the hearts of Australian racing fans, by the New Sydney Showground Speedway.

Upper photo: Allan Gerard

Lower photo: Bruce Craig

Ray Revell
Clive Martin
Kev Gallaher
Dinny Patterson

Fort Erie, Ontario, Canada

The first auto race in Canada was held September 26, 1901 on the one mile dirt Fort Erie horse track under the sponsorship of the Buffalo, New York, Auto Club. The site is just west of the Niagara River opposite Buffalo and about 20 miles upstream from Niagara Falls. Henry Fournier, "the great French automobilist" took the day's honors in a Morse with a time of 31 minutes, 58 and 2/5 seconds for 30 laps, considered at the time a world's record on a mile track. Other competing vehicles included five steam locomobiles and one White, a Napier, three Packards, three Wintons, a Duryea and an Apperson.

There were also races for motorcycles and steam cars.

In 2001 Fort Erie recognized the 100th anniversary of the race and Robert Deull of the Canadian Motor Racing Historical Society presented the city a plaque marking the event. Races were held at Fort Erie until 1910; it was then used as a practice track for the adjacent active horse race track. In 2002 the overgrown outline of the 1901 course may still be seen.

Map: 1950

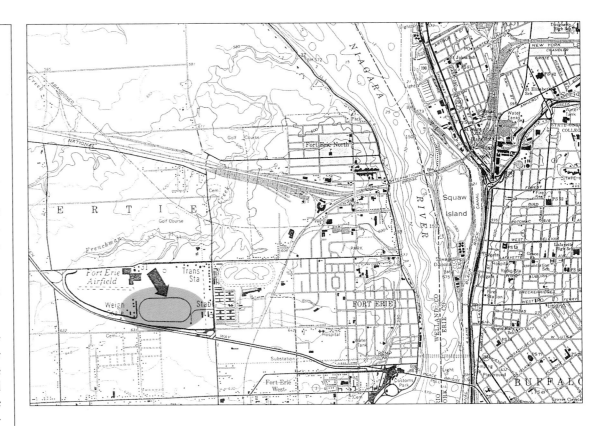

120

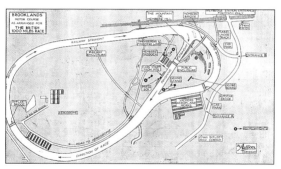

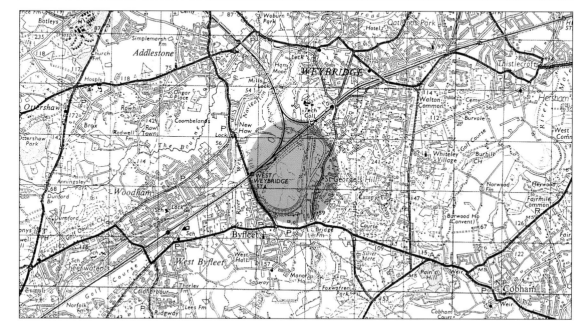

Brooklands Motor Course, England

The Brooklands track, a 3 1/4-mile oval, was the British Indianapolis, built two years before the Hoosier oval. It was designed by a wealthy developer as a test ground for early automobile manufacturers. The infield, as was the case at Minneapolis and Atlanta in the U.S., became an airfield. It was taken over entirely in 1914 by the Royal Air Force, but returned to racing in 1920.

During the 1930s many record runs were made there, including a 135 mph lap by Gwenda Glubb Stewart in this ex-Red Shafer Miller front-drive (with a propellor-driven oil pump!)

In WW II Brooklands was not so lucky. Taken again by the RAF the track was cut to lengthen the Vickers Aeroplane Works runway and it was bombed by the Luftwaffe. In 1946 the Labour Government declined to make repairs and the stockholders, including Sir Malcolm Campbell, decided to sell the property as industrial real estate for 330,000 pounds.

Today part of the Railway Banking remains and a museum occupies one of the WW II hangers.

Photos: Author's Collection
Map: 1940

Reims Grand Prix Circuit, France

The Reims, France, Grand Prix circuit was first used in 1925. A 9.5 kilometer paved course over public roads, it replaced Monthlery as the site of the French Grand Prix beginning in 1932, a race won by Tazio Nuvolari. In 1952 the track was shortened to 8.34 kilometers and improved until it was the fastest in Europe. Financial problems led to its downfall and the last French Grand Prix was held there in 1966 and the track closed in 1969. The tribunes and other buildings still existed in 2002, but are extremely dilapidated and are expected to be torn down soon.

Photo: Paul Hooft

Diagram: 1966

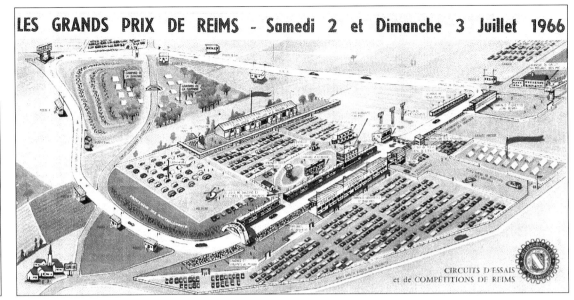

LES GRANDS PRIX DE REIMS - Samedi 2 et Dimanche 3 Juillet 1966

CIRCUITS D'ESSAIS et de COMPÉTITIONS DE REIMS

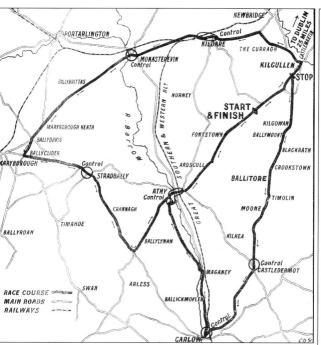

Gordon Bennett Race Course, Ireland

In 1898 James Gordon Bennett, publisher of the *New York Herald,* established a trophy and a prize fund for a series of annual international motor races. The British won the 1902 race in France with a Napier and thus the right to host the 1903 event, but were barred by law from using English roads. The Irish Parliament passed a bill permitting use of their highways for a day.

Organizers laid out a 92.75-mile heart-shaped course 25 miles southwest of Dublin, over which competitors ran three and a half laps or 368 miles.

The American hope, Alexander Winton, seen here in Winton Bullet No. 2 as he prepared to start the race, broke down and withdrew. Camille Jenatzy, the "Red Devil," won the race in a 60 hp Mercedes.

Photo: Smithsonian

Map: 1902

Monza Autodromo, Italy

The Circuite Automobilist di Milano was built in 1922 originally as a banked oval of 2.79 miles with a 10 kilometer road course. Pietro Bordino won the first race on September 1st in a Fiat. Speeds began to exceed the capability of the track and a 1928 crash killed driver Emilio Materassi and 27 spectators. In 1929 American Leon Duray drove his Miller 91 on the *Autodrome* at speeds near 141 mph. In 1934 new circuits were laid out of varying distances and in 1939 parts of the high banks were demolished and a 3.9 mile road course installed.

A parade of Allied armored vehicles in 1945 broke up much of the 1939 track. A full-scale rebuilding was carried out in 1955, essentially restoring the original 1922 design with a 2.5 mile banked speedway or *Autodromo*. In celebration, the City of Monza invited the American Indianapolis roadsters there in the "Race of Two Worlds," won in 1957 by Jimmy Bryan and in 1958 by Jim Rathmann.

The death of Wolfgang Von Trips and 11 spectators in the 1961 Italian Grand Prix led to abandoning the high speed oval for Grand Prix racing, and later for any serious running. It was due to be substantially demolished by 2003.

Photos: Phil Harms

Map: 1926

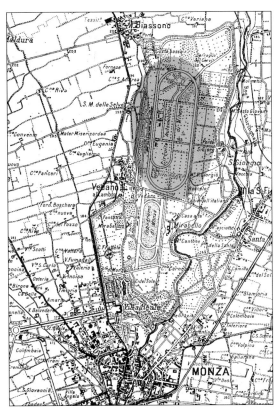

Carrera Panamericana, Mexico

The Carrera Panamericana, the Mexican Road Race, was planned originally as a one-time affair to celebrate the completion of the Pan American Highway in Mexico. It went on for four more years, a grueling five-day, 1,908-mile run up the Highway from Textla Gutierrez just north of the Guatamalan border, through Mexico City to Juarez at the U.S. line. Elevations ranged from near sea level to more than 10,400 feet.

Winners included Chuck Stevenson, the AAA national champion, in 1952 and 1953 in stock Lincolns prepared by Bill Stroppe and Clay Smith, Ray Crawford in another Lincoln in 1954 and Karl Kling in a Mercedes 300SL in the sports car class in 1953. Seen here is Jack Ensley's Kurtis 500S finishing the first leg at Oaxaca in 1953.

The 1955 race was canceled after several deaths in earlier years and the 1955 Le Mans tragedy, combined with the inconvenience of closing the highway to regular traffic and charges and countercharges of corruption over financing of the Carrera.

Photo: IMRRC, Watkins Glen
Map: ANA

Il Carrera Panamericana "MEXICO"

Tuxtla Gutierrez–C. Juárez

EPILOGUE

Of the more than 8,200 motor racing courses that have existed in the United States, 7,000 have disappeared entirely or have been turned to other uses, as horse tracks, public roads, outdoor music festivals, shopping centers, housing, airports, industrial sites and parking lots. Few race tracks have had extensive, expensive structures to them and many that did, like the board tracks, succumbed to fire or weather. It is easy to replace a race track.

Even where tracks have been financially successful the encroachment of homes and businesses and the accompanying complaints about noise and dust have brought many down. There seems no way to guarantee the life of a race track. Only the Indianapolis Motor Speedway seems immune from financial or physical decay or the complaints of neighbors.

Time moves on, styles and habits change. Sic transit gloria mundi.

Gordon Eliot White, 2002

MORE TITLES FROM ICONOGRAFIX

*This product is sold under license from Mack Trucks, Inc. Mack is a registered Trademark of Mack Trucks, Inc. All rights reserved.

All Iconografix books are available from direct mail specialty book dealers and bookstores worldwide, or can be ordered from the publisher.
For book trade and distribution information or to add your name to our mailing list and receive a **FREE CATALOG** contact:

Iconografix, PO Box 446, Dept BK, Hudson, Wisconsin, 54016   Telephone: (715) 381-9755, (800) 289-3504 (USA), Fax: (715) 381-9756

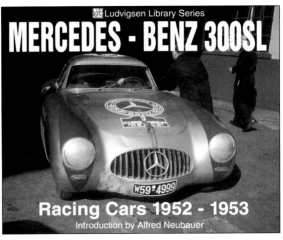

Ludvigsen Library Series

MERCEDES - BENZ 300SL

Racing Cars 1952 - 1953

Introduction by Alfred Neubauer

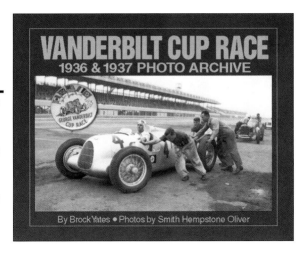

VANDERBILT CUP RACE
1936 & 1937 PHOTO ARCHIVE

By Brock Yates • Photos by Smith Hempstone Oliver

MORE
GREAT BOOKS
FROM ICONOGRAFIX

**MERCEDES-BENZ 300SL RACING CARS 1952-1953
LUDVIGSEN LIBRARY SERIES**
ISBN 1-58388-067-4

**VANDERBILT CUP RACE 1936 & 1937 PHOTO
ARCHIVE** ISBN 1-882256-66-2

**INDIANAPOLIS RACING CARS OF FRANK KURTIS
1941-1963 PHOTO ARCHIVE**
ISBN 1-58388-026-7

**NOVI V-8 INDY CARS 1941-1965 LUDVIGSEN
LIBRARY SERIES** ISBN 1-58388-037-2

**INDY CARS OF THE 1950s, LUDVIGSEN LIBRARY
SERIES** ISBN 1-58388-018-6

**DRAG RACING FUNNY CARS OF THE 1970s PHOTO
ARCHIVE** ISBN 1-58388-068-2

**INDY CARS OF THE 1960s, LUDVIGSEN LIBRARY
SERIES** ISBN 1-58388-052-6

**ICONOGRAFIX, INC.
P.O. BOX 446, DEPT BK,
HUDSON, WI 54016
FOR A FREE CATALOG CALL:
1-800-289-3504**

INDIANAPOLIS RACING CARS
of FRANK KURTIS
1941 - 1963 PHOTO ARCHIVE

Gordon Eliot White

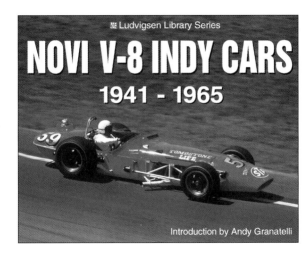

Ludvigsen Library Series

NOVI V-8 INDY CARS
1941 - 1965

Introduction by Andy Granatelli

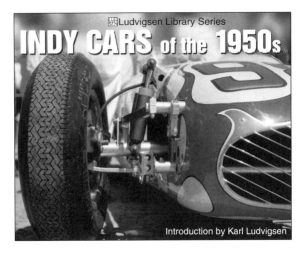

Ludvigsen Library Series

INDY CARS of the 1950s

Introduction by Karl Ludvigsen

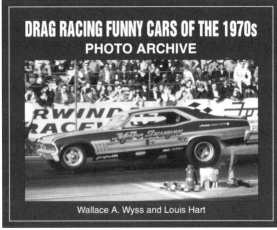

DRAG RACING FUNNY CARS OF THE 1970s
PHOTO ARCHIVE

Wallace A. Wyss and Louis Hart

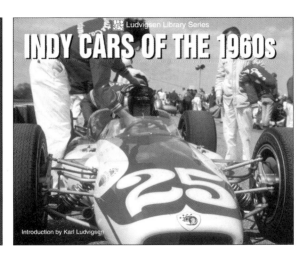

Ludvigsen Library Series

INDY CARS OF THE 1960s

Introduction by Karl Ludvigsen